T0342238

PIVOTS, PATTERNS, AND INTRADAY SWING TRADES

PIVOTS, PATTERNS, AND INTRADAY SWING TRADES

Derivatives Analysis with the E-mini
and Russell Futures Contracts

M. William Scheier
ValhallaFutures.com

WILEY

Cover Design: Wiley
Cover Image: ©iStockphoto.com / epic11

All charts wherein courtesy of Ninjatrader.com
All data courtesy of Kinetic, a subsidiary of Ninjatrader.com
Published simultaneously in Canada.

For general information on our other products and services or for technical support, please contact
our Customer Care Department within the United States at (800) 762-2974, outside the United
States at (317) 572-3993 or fax (317) 572-4002.

Wiley publishes in a variety of print and electronic formats and by print-on-demand. Some material
included with standard print versions of this book may not be included in e-books or in print-
on-demand. If this book refers to media such as a CD or DVD that is not included in the version
you purchased, you may download this material at http://booksupport.wiley.com. For more
information about Wiley products, visit www.wiley.com.

Library of Congress Cataloging-in-Publication Data:
Scheier, M. William.
  Pivots, patterns and intraday swing trades : derivatives analysis with the e-mini and Russell
futures contracts / M. William Scheier.
       pages cm. – (Wiley trading series)
  Includes bibliographical references and index.
  ISBN 978-1-118-77579-0 (cloth); ISBN 978-1-118-77586-8 (ebk);
ISBN 978-1-118-77584-4 (ebk)
  1. Technical analysis (Investment analysis) 2. Speculation. 3. Stocks–Charts, diagrams, etc.
4. Derivative securities. I. Title.
  HG4529.S35 2014
  332.64'5–dc23

                                                                                    2013038867

Printed in the United States of America

10 9 8 7 6 5 4 3 2 1

Dedicated to the memory of Randolph Newman,
and to his wonderful granddaughter Glenny,
who saw in me something of merit
when I was a young man.

CONTENTS

Preface   xi

PART ONE   TIME FRAME CONCEPTS

CHAPTER 1   **A Three-Frame Day**   3

The 1st Frame   6
The Midday Frame   8
The Last Hour Time Frame   9
Summary   11
Notes   11

CHAPTER 2   **Opening Range Bar**   13

ORB Defined   13
3-Bar ORB   15
ORB Pennant   17
ORB Matched Highs/Lows   20
Summary   21
Notes   22

CHAPTER 3   **Pivot/Exhaustion Grid**   23

ORB Kilroy   24
Break-Away Pivots: The Pivot Ledge   27
The Break-Away Lap   28
Previous Highs and Lows   31
Previous Closing Prices: The Gap   34
Tick Bar Laps   35

Dynamic Exhaustion Levels: The EMAs   37

Floor Trader's Pivot Points   40

Fibonacci Targets   41

Measured Move Targets   43

Market Profile   43

Trend Lines   44

Summary   46

Notes   46

CHAPTER 4   Dough Bar to Die Bar   49

Summary   54

CHAPTER 5   Leadership Divergence   55

Summary   62

CHAPTER 6   The Work-Done Concept   63

Summary   67

CHAPTER 7   Trading the News   69

Summary   76

Notes   77

PART TWO   DAY MODEL PATTERNS

CHAPTER 8   Persistent Trend Day   81

Persistence in Trend: It's a Thing   82

ORB Entries   85

Telltale Leadership   85

Leadership Shift   87

Flubber Bounce/Monkey Bars   89

Last Chance Texaco: The 200EMA Entry   91

Summary   93

Notes   93

CHAPTER 9   Test-and-Reject Day   95

Summary   101

Notes   101

CHAPTER 10   The Split-Open Day   103

Summary   104

Notes   104

CHAPTER 11   Day Model Sequence Cycle   105

             Summary   111
             Notes   112

         PART THREE   Repetitive Chart Patterns

CHAPTER 12   The Momentum Grid   115

             Summary   119
             Notes   120

CHAPTER 13   Pre-Breakout Pause Pattern   121

             Summary   124

CHAPTER 14   The Classics Revisited   125

             M-Tops, W-Bottoms   126
             Telltale Triangles   127
             Head-and-Shoulders Reversals, Revised   131
             The Rising/Declining Wedge   134
             Midday Channel   136
             Summary   139
             Notes   140

CHAPTER 15   MA Pattern Concepts   141

             The EMA Pinch   141
             Gap-Close . . . or Further?   143
             The EMA Cup   144
             The Cup as Breakout Trigger   146
             Summary   147

         PART FOUR   Confluence and Execution

CHAPTER 16   Transition Time Reversals   151

             Summary   156

CHAPTER 17   Trade Entry Models   157

             Summary   172

CHAPTER 18   The Trade Plan   173

             Prescript   174
             Blueprint   176
             My Blueprint Notes   179
             Summary   183

APPENDIX A   Companion Website   185

APPENDIX B   Color Legend   187

APPENDIX C   Serial Sequent Wave Method   191

APPENDIX D   ValhallaFutures Indicator Package
and Intraday Index Futures Trading Course   195

APPENDIX E   Screen Capturing an Event Library   197

APPENDIX F   Randolph Newman   199

APPENDIX G   Fibonacci versus Pivot/Exhaustion Grid   203

APPENDIX H   The Last Triangle   207

Bibliography   209

About the Author   213

Index   215

M y initial efforts in trading were focused almost exclusively on what is known as *position trading*, using equities and the physical commodity futures. Stretched out over the days and weeks a position could last, a trend in that time frame would eventually begin to make sense in technical terms, unfolding gradually as it proceeded on. There was a pace to the decision process. As a trader, one could mull over the conflicting elements of the technical picture. Some aspects would recede into the background and render themselves less relevant; some would grow in their importance and become glaring.

Initial forays into day trading stock index futures reveal a starkly different decision environment. There is no time to dwell on technical conditions. A day trade opportunity does not take shape over days and weeks. Opposing technical signals don't recede in time enough to sweep away the cross current of doubts before a decision is required. By the time a trend finally makes sense, it is often about to end. Intraday volatility in the stock indices is far more exaggerated than the daily bar charts of other markets, partly due to the extreme leverage, partly due to the intense participation. And positioning techniques that survive in the action of the long-term trends in other instruments get slaughtered in the countertrend reactions of the highly leveraged S&P 500 futures contract within the short term.

When starting out, understanding the day as it unfolded on a day trading scale was akin to trying to read a foreign language or decipher a secret code. Somehow the tremendous opportunities in these intraday trend swings were surely being captured successfully, but by whom?

The less-experienced student will often assume that floor traders in the pit capture the intraday swings. After all, those guys must be in the know. Their access is so immediate. They literally create price. That being out there—hanging 10 on the leading edge to the rhythm of history—must provide a better view, and information not otherwise available to the rest of us must be streaming across the pit at critical moments, providing the insight to decipher the head fakes from the real trend swings. One could easily come to the conclusion that because these guys are the professionals, they must surely make up that slim minority who are consistently taking the profits from those less skilled working off-floor on their video screens.

But nothing could be further from the truth. Floor traders are, for the most part, scalpers. They tend to front-run or fade the order flow. To them, swing trading intraday trends *would* be position trading. I was also surprised to learn that the majority of floor traders see the world from the point of view of Efficient Market Theorists, admittedly or not. For floor traders, if paper flow into the pit is the current of energy driving the markets, then it is the news and news events that provide the power supply for that energy. Why should they believe otherwise, given their worldview!

Nor is the S&P pit in Chicago the bastion of capitalism and free trade one might think it to be. The number of Efficient Market Practitioners on the floor of the futures exchange is only surpassed by the number of pit traders whose politics reveal an inclination toward unionism, trade regulation, intervention, and controls. Remarks from otherwise very talented traders actually reveal the belief that it was one U.S. President's tenure or another that caused a difficult period of market activity or a particularly beneficial one. With thinking like that underlying the operations of the S&P pit, how much insight is to be garnered there for a conceptual understanding of market trend structure? The theory of Random Walk never had more adamant proponents.

A useful propensity toward trend analysis was already working for me when I approached day trading—that of pattern recognition. What was needed to crack the code of intraday trend disguise was to see the process of pattern recognition in broader terms than just visual price formation. What was needed was an expanded understanding of pattern recognition to include other concepts in market behavior, concepts of technical event minutia, including time of day and relative price position, especially those happening in tandem. From such concepts, models were derived, and with models, the activity of an otherwise indecipherable and random-looking day could be matched to one or more of a limited number of codified categories, each replete with its own setups.

The application of this broader definition of pattern recognition is particularly well adapted to the shorter time frames, where the decision environment requires quick response. When Adrian De Groot, a psychologist working in the 1960s, studied the differences between chess players, he discovered that the grandmasters recognized familiar configurations and visual patterns to assess game progress and decipher board strategy; they did not rely on mathematics, statistics, or remarkable memory skills. How else could a single player manage to play dozens of games simultaneously, going from board to board with near immediate response!

The focus of this book is day trading in the shorter time frames of the stock index futures contracts, with techniques that are anything but mechanical scalping. With conceptual event models and their accompanying rules, the intent is to convey a set of tools by which the major intraday swing trends can be identified quickly, and often at the very turning points where they begin.

The voice of the text is directed at the trading community in general, with an intentional clarity for each explanation aimed at the beginner stock index futures trader in particular. The term *Trader* has been capitalized in many places as a reference to the profile of a specific role model intended for emulation by any man or woman who understands that the process of development is ever one of student to market, and not one of retail to professional.

PIVOTS, PATTERNS, AND INTRADAY SWING TRADES

PART ONE

TIME FRAME CONCEPTS

"Everybody" is always wrong. If everyone was right and no one was wrong, "everybody" would be rich and nobody would be poor. "Everybody" is always wrong.

—Randolph Newman[1]

Even the scholar most in repute knows only what is reputed and holds fast to just that.

—Heraclitus

CHAPTER 1

A Three-Frame Day

For the longest time as a commodities position trader, I was confused by day trading, especially day trading the S&P 500 futures contract. The lengthy trading period of nearly seven hours was itself an impediment to understanding the price action. The day's trading behavior patterns and events often seemed strung together at random, encouraging the deceptive practice of attributing trend direction to unfolding news events. There was no making any technical sense of it from one hour to the next. But it cleared up almost immediately when I began to view the day as divided into three separate and distinct trading sessions: the *1st Frame*, the *Midday Frame*, and the 3rd or *Last Hour Time Frame*.

These are just names. In truth, the periods don't last for exactly the same time each day. The 1st Frame of the day can last about 1 hour and 45 minutes, give or take about 20 minutes. The Midday Frame can last anywhere from about three to about three-and-a-half hours. And the Last Hour Time Frame gets whatever is left over, occasionally not distinguishing itself at all. Although traders often refer to this third period as the "last hour," I have found it to begin earlier and extend longer than the last hour of the trading day.

To be of any practical use, however, these time periods should be treated as fixed. In that way, a rule-based approach can serve to compare daily action in the transition windows from one period to the next. Each of these three main periods of the trading day does, in fact, have a flavor and unique character all its own. Because price action actually changes in character from one period to the next, and does so fairly consistently, different methods to trade these different behavior periods serve better than a one-size-fits-all plan. Rules can be devised based on the differences between these time sessions, and thus can help reduce one's temptation to introduce into trade entry decisions the intuition that rules of a trade plan are designed to eliminate. So for purposes of establishing a time reminder, and a trigger to implement a different phase of a trading plan, the 1st Frame of the day for the equity indices starts from the cash opening of the New York Stock Exchange at 9:30 A.M. and lasts until 11:15 A.M. ET. The Midday Frame picks up at that point and extends to 2:30 P.M. And, thereafter, the Last Hour Time Frame of the day starts at 2:30 P.M. and extends until the futures close at 4:15 P.M. ET, 15 minutes past the NYSE cash equity close.

An important thing not to confuse about these three time periods is the association with trend. Going from one time period to another does not necessarily mean a change of trend, although it can. Instead, it is better to understand the transition from frame to frame in terms of *resolution*, *momentum*, *price action*, and *complexity of pattern*.

Often, one time period can be said to be a resolution to the one preceding it. The 1st Frame of the day is usually the more volatile, and thus the Midday Frame tends to consolidate what was accomplished in the earlier going. If, instead, the 1st Frame is corrective and overlapping in pattern, more like a consolidation pattern, it usually resolves itself early in the Midday Frame by a sharp breakout into trend. However, when analyzing the relationship between the first two frames, the latter pattern occurs less often. The 1st Frame is usually the more volatile and trending, and the Midday Frame tends more to consolidate or even just chop around. If the Midday Frame builds a consolidation pattern, it will usually resolve itself in transition to the Last Hour Time Frame, beginning around 2:30 P.M. ET. If the trend in one period is destined to continue into the next, it will often accelerate in transition. If a trend had already accelerated within one time period, the next period may see a slowdown and even become choppy. Reversals can come in the middle of any period, but the momentum and the direction of such a reversal is more likely to change around 11:15 A.M. or 2:30 P.M. Short-term reversals are especially common at 10:30 A.M. and 12 P.M., and are thus also worthy to be included as designated *Time Markers*, but the transition of momentum and price action is better represented at the specific Time Markers of 11:15 P.M. and 2:30 P.M. ET.

Marking at least these two *Transition Times* on your own charts every day is a great exercise. Watch how often the market action seems to call for either a trade exit or entry as they approach. (See Figures 1.1 and 1.2.)

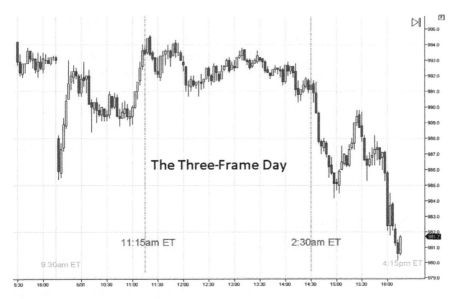

The Three-Frame Day

9:30am ET   11:15am ET   2:30am ET   4:15pm ET

FIGURE 1.1   Transition Times

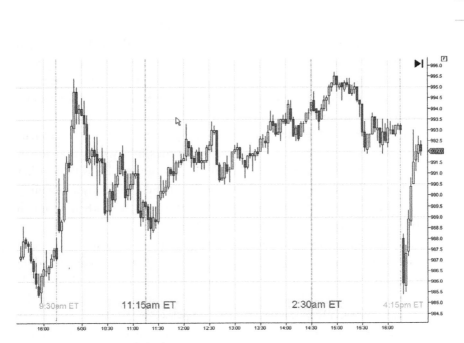

9:30am ET   11:15am ET   2:30am ET   4:15pm ET

FIGURE 1.2   Transition Times

(For colorized versions of these charts, go to the Wiley companion website for this book, with instructions in Appendix A).

To be an effective trader, plotting such lines of time frame demarcation must become more than an exercise of mere curiosity. It must become habitual. And speaking from a lot of experience, traders can become lazy and complacent. Besides, in the heat of a trade entry or exit decision, many other emotional factors can take precedence over something a trader may or may not remember to check. Therefore, an indicator that automatically plots vertical lines on the screen at these critical junctures should be a standard tool in a trader's software package.[2]

■ The 1st Frame

While stock investors and position traders often consider the closing price of each day to be the most important for assessing performance, day traders consider the opening price as the most critical, as Grant Noble has noted in his book, *The Trader's Edge*.[3] Everything that happens for the entire day in the futures market—and especially price reaction throughout the first hour—is influenced by that opening. Volume and volatility are usually strongest in this first time period.

Pent-up orders from traders and institutions alike arrive at the floor most heavily at the opening bell, 9:30 A.M. ET. Attendance in the S&P and Nasdaq trading pits on the floor of the Chicago Mercantile Exchange is always greatest during this period. So important is the 1st Frame time period that many of these same floor traders consider the day over when the first hour and a half or so comes to an end.

For beginning traders, the opening hour presents some special challenges. Price volatility can be extreme, sometimes in a whipsaw manner. This volatility can frustrate the placement of stop-loss orders, as the market seems almost determined to take them out. Then again, on many a morning, price action seems truncated, sometimes on the very days when so much direction would have otherwise been expected.

That is why many novice traders get chopped up in the early going, and are warned to avoid trading in the first hour. Without a specific trading methodology that takes into account where the day's pivots and reversals are most likely to take place, a trader hoping to initiate a position for the early trend is not likely to survive his first stop-loss order.

Think about what was said earlier in this section regarding the S&P trading pit attendance. Some floor traders are done for the day after the 1st Frame is over. That means they've managed to accomplish their trading goals without a care as to where the market ends up for the day. When it opens again tomorrow, they'll have the same opportunity they had today. The price levels will be different, and they'll have a different set of numbers to work with, but for them, with their short-term worldview, the opportunity will be just the same.

If you come from investing in stocks, or even commodity position trading with holding periods of several days, weeks, or even months, the thought of viewing the first hour as almost an entire session unto itself is almost jarring. But if you want to be successful trading the stock index contracts, the 1st Frame should be understood exactly that way.

Think of the market hour that comes just previous to the beginning of the Midday Frame as one of testing. Only on rare occasions does the market know exactly where it is going from the very beginning. Think of this period as vying for dominance of trend direction between two warring factions.

Some of the largest players, like funds, have been compelled to commit dollars for various reasons; some have been forced to withdraw them. Some are reacting to the events of the previous day or fresh news; some are anticipating those of the day to follow. But by the end of the 1st Frame session, the result of this exchange has left the market in a position to commit to direction. By this hour's end, on a great majority of days, as was the case in Figure 1.3, one end of the entire day's trading range has already been established.

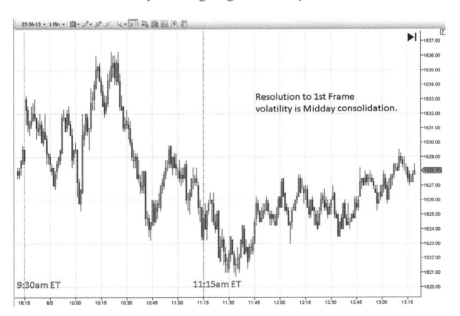

FIGURE 1.3 **Midday Frame Transition**

■ The Midday Frame

The Midday Frame starts at 11:15 A.M. ET, as the morning rush to commit funds begins to subside. Many seasoned floor traders who have been actively trading the morning's volatile swings are ready to leave for a break not long after this period begins. Some are even leaving for the day. If the market action has been volatile up to this time, action often now begins to be choppy, and that means entry signals and techniques can get sloppy for the trader who has waited till now to take a position.

It's as if the price action of the 1st Frame has left a kind of watermark on the page, a footprint pointing in the sand, a pencil rubbing of the struggle just beneath the surface. The task for the Trader in this period of transition is to recognize that the first of the day's major battles is probably over, and even if the current trend is not over, to consider taking no fresh trades while this transition period takes hold. A new trend or even a major reversal may be at hand, but at the very minimum, it's time to take a fresh appraisal of the situation.

After that, as shown in Figure 1.4, a trend has completed. The pace begins to slow down, and price patterns become more complex. The Midday Frame has then begun to develop. Breakouts usually begin to lose their

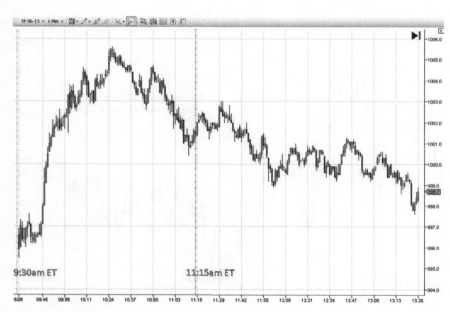

FIGURE 1.4 Midday Frame Transition

energy and often fizzle. What might have been a simple 3-bar pause pattern in the 1st Frame now shows up as a 10-bar Elliott *abc* pattern. Where price can—and often does—pivot on a single bar in the first hour, it is apt to form more complex, even classical chart reversal patterns later in the day. This is the time when the market usually begins to consolidate, and trade strategies that don't account for this potential change of pace and pattern are usually doomed to failure.

A beginner trader often finds the opportunity of the first hour irresistible, but the pace so furious that it's already over before he even has a sense of the trend that finally takes place. So, he waits until things slow down in the Midday Frame. Too often, the less experienced trader comes into the market at that point intending to capture in the Midday Frame what he missed in the 1st Frame's trend. This is usually disastrous. The character of the action following the Midday Frame transition begins to settle down. The position he takes in the Midday Frame with the 1st Frame's action in mind proves mismatched to the change of pace and market behavior that has begun to occur as the Midday Frame takes over.

The Midday Frame is usually a new ball game altogether. You can't capture what was missed in the 1st Frame with trades taken in the Midday Frame. The 1st Frame period is over. The Midday Frame models are different. Strategies for the Midday Frame must take into consideration a change of pace and an added complexity to the setups. Since each period stands on its own merits, each period must be traded by its own models and corresponding rules.

Although this change in volatility is fairly consistent, nothing is without its exceptions. This one, however, is consistent enough that its absence becomes an important signal of its own. Section Two, about Day Model Patterns, covers trend signals that can occur by just observing the character of transition from the 1st Frame to the Midday Frame.

■ The Last Hour Time Frame

The 3rd period, or Last Hour Time Frame, begins at 2:30 P.M. and lasts until the futures markets close at 4:15 P.M. ET, 15 minutes after the close of the New York Stock Exchange cash market. By 2:30 P.M., many traders who were away for the Midday Frame have returned to the floor. The corrective patterns that defined the Midday Frame have now possibly consolidated into an identifying whole.

It is here that many a day's trend either reasserts the direction of the morning, or is slaughtered by a reversal of the day's early action. The beginning of this time period is usually the resolution to the consolidation or coiling of the previous frame. So consistent is the change of action between the Midday Frame and the Last Hour Time Frame that this Time Marker warrants a name of its own: the *2:30 Transition Time*.

When fast-breaking action again ensues, patterns that took 30 minutes to set up in the Midday Frame now barely take five or six in Last Hour action. And if this period sounds like it might be the easiest to act on—following the methodical setup of a familiar Midday breakout pattern—the trader should keep one thing in mind. The outcome of any given day's Last Hour Time Frame is often the biggest surprise to the majority of traders. Note the chart in Figure 1.5 continues the day shown in Figure 1.3.

If, on the other hand, it was the Midday Frame that did the trending instead of the more usual consolidation, then the yin yang flips again and the 2:30 Transition Time can bring an end to the Midday Frame trend and serve to consolidate or reverse.

Notice how the chart in Figure 1.6 is a continuation of the day in Figure 1.4.

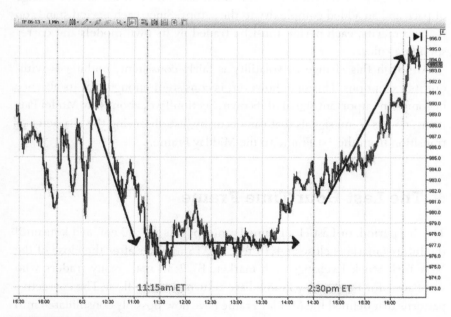

FIGURE 1.5 Last Hour Transition

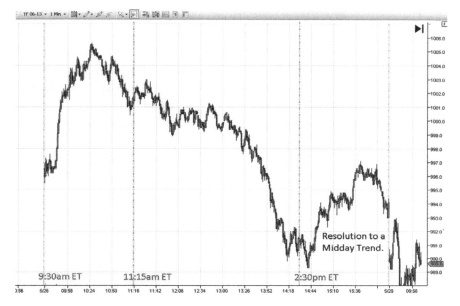

FIGURE 1.6 2:30 P.M. Transition Time

◼ Summary

Dividing the day into separate time frames or sessions would seem arbitrary and without authority. No bells are rung, nor are any exchange notifications published at the above-designated times. But the experience of daily observation teaches that there are definitely transitions of price behavior at certain times day after day. The novice trader wants an explanation for these phenomena: end of the bond market, end of the energy markets, muscle memory from the occasional Federal Reserve interest rate announcements, and so forth. The novice trader wants logic. But the market is not driven by logic. None of these proposed reasons really fit. The experienced Trader doesn't care. He is only interested in market behavior that repeats itself with enough regularity to give him an edge to his trading. Leave the logic for the Analyst. Be the Trader.

◼ Notes

1. Among the stages in his lifetime career as a trader, Randy was a floor broker at the New Orleans Cotton Exchange and, in his final years, my mentor while I was but a young man. For a more complete biography of Randolph Newman, see Appendix F.

2. There are so many charting software packages in use among the huge pool of traders worldwide that it's impractical to offer code for such indicators within this book. However, the code for automatic vertical plots of these two frame Transition Times, as well as auto-plot lines for the 10:30 A.M. and 12 P.M. times, is available as a Time Marker indicator in the ValhallaFutures Indicator Package, valhallafutures.com.

3. Grant Noble, *The Trader's Edge* (Chicago, IL: Probus Publishing, McGraw-Hill, 1994).

CHAPTER 2

Opening Range Bar

I know of some very successful day traders who avoid the first hour altogether. I've even heard it referred to it as *amateur hour*. Perhaps for swing traders and fund managers who hold positions overnight and are trying to avoid being trapped in gap-opening reversals this is true. But for most intraday traders and almost all floor traders, the opposite is actually the case. The 1st Frame is when the professionals trade.

In fact, some of the best traders I have ever met focus almost exclusively on the opening time period, and some even leave the market for the rest of the day after the 1st Frame is over. Considering the hours, it's not a bad life, if you can make it work. With the series of figures and text in this section, I'll examine some of the methods a day trader working from his video screen can employ to capture the earliest trends of the day.

■ ORB Defined

In truth, there is no such thing as the Opening Range Bar (ORB). It's a sort of manufactured item. But there is a thing called the Opening Range. If you've ever listened to a squawk box from the S&P pit, you'll have heard it called out by the pit boss shortly after the NYSE cash opening, just after 9:30 A.M. ET. Orders have piled up overnight and before the actual cash opening so that they can be crossed at a time when there's enough offsetting volume. It usually takes less than a minute for these orders to be offset, but when they finally are, the price range for this initial auction is pegged as the Opening Range.

But we trade in the electronic world. The exchanges for the mini-index futures contracts are in computer servers, not open-outcry pits. So we approximate the Opening Range and use the first 1-minute time bar of the day as our Opening Range Bar, or O-R-B. This small range is the first and most important support/resistance number for the entire day. We bracket this range bar and leave the lines of this bracket on our charts for the rest of the day. Stock traders talk in terms of being "green" or "red" on the day in accordance with whether prices are above or below yesterday's Close, the Y-Close. But for futures traders, prices are said to be down or up from the Open, and the Y-Close is just another support/resistance number to be potentially used as a trade entry or exit point, albeit a fairly important one. (See Figure 2.1.)

Normally, when points of support and resistance are hit by price once or twice during the day, it is wise to remove any line plot associated with their price level from the charts. In fact, most support/resistance numbers are used once, and thrown away. But with the ORB, its relevance to trade entries, exits, Day Models, and overall trend direction remains active throughout the rest of the day. So after drawing lines to bracket the ORB, we leave them up all day—but only to the end of the day—and start again fresh each morning at the Open with a new bracket of line plots.

Not only does the ORB remain a support/resistance zone even after tested by price, but it also seems to regain its power if price vacates the range for a few hours before returning. It's as if it recuperated in the absence of attention. In

The Opening Range as support and resistance throughout the day.

FIGURE 2.1 Opening Range as Support and Resistance throughout the Day

later chapters where Midday Frame action is being discussed, more examples of the ORB concept will be demonstrated, especially one called Kilroy's Castle.

The market can be erratic at its Open, and a departure in one direction or another away from the ORB initially means little as to the trend direction of the day. There are, nonetheless, several trade setups we derive from bar patterns that develop immediately after the opening that usually do produce tradable trends. Whole schools of methodology have evolved around Opening Range Breakouts. Toby Crabel's *Day Trading with Short Term Price Patterns and Opening Range Breakout*, was the first to gain notoriety.[1] Larry Williams used a similar method of back-testing rule-based patterns and combined the models with day-of-week seasonality as a further filter.[2] But I have found both these methods inconsistent, despite the hefty price tag Toby Crabel's collectors-only book now fetches.

What follows are three ORB price patterns that do produce successful breakouts with a very high degree of consistency. Although none occur more than one or twice a month, I watch for each of them every day. A successful breakout trade usually gets my account well on its way toward a minimum daily profit goal within the first few minutes of trading. And unlike those models of Crabel and Williams fame, these patterns are not derived from daily price bars, and therefore can occur independently of what happened yesterday or the day before. Each day is a fresh opportunity for these to reappear.

■ 3-Bar ORB

The rules for the 3-Bar at the ORB are simple but very precise. This pattern model sets up immediately after the opening, so the rules must be memorized to be quickly recognized before the third minute arrives. Oddly enough, when I teach this pattern to new students, they don't take to heart the precision of the rules, and often attempt the trade after setup-rule violations.

Using the first three, 1-minute bars of the opening, compare their respective highs and lows. For a bull breakout, each of the successive bars must have a lower low and lower high. If the fourth bar breaks the low of the third bar, the setup is violated. Just reverse this pattern into three higher highs and higher lows for a bear setup. In the leftmost chart of the two displayed in Figure 2.2, from June 6, 2013, note that the directional color and candle pattern of the bars can vary between the three bars without voiding the setup. (Colorized version of Figure 2.2 is available on the Wiley companion website. See Appendix A for access instructions.)

The entry trigger assumes it's a reversal pattern, and is placed as a buy-stop order one tick beyond the middle of the three down-trending bars, positioning for a potential breakout in the opposite direction to the mini-trend of the three

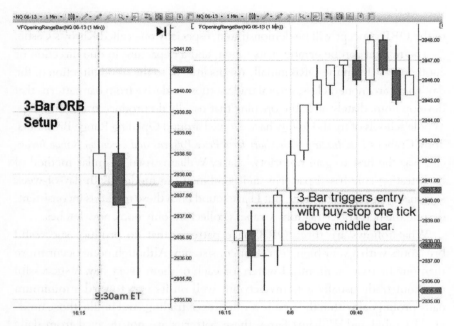

FIGURE 2.2 3-Bar ORB Bear Setup, with Breakout

bars themselves. Beginners please note: Once triggered, the success of a trade is one of position management. With a two-unit position, exit one unit quickly, with as little as 0.4 points in the mini Russell contract (symbol TF), 7 points in the mini-Dow (YM), and 1.75 points in the E-mini NASDAQ (NQ). Move the stop-loss on the second unit to an amount of risk comparable to this initial small profit. If the breakout fails, chances are still high that this initial unit exit target will have been filled with enough profit to cover the loss of the surviving unit. A position unit is any fixed number of contracts suitable for a trader's own risk tolerance. For beginning traders, one unit equals just one contract.

The pattern works in both directions. For bear trend breakdowns, the bars make successive higher highs and higher lows. Again, the rules are precise. Students typically ignore the precision at their expense. The bars must overlap and be limited to just three in the direction of this miniature trend. Occasionally, the first three bars fall or rise too sharply, one stacked on top of the other without overlapping. This, too, invalidates the setup. Note in Figure 2.3, from May 29, 2013, how the chart on the left was a valid *bear* setup, but the chart on the right was an invalid *bull* setup.

Although this opening pattern can be seen in any contract, I never use it to trade the E-mini S&P (symbol ES). It can work satisfactorily in the

FIGURE 2.3 Valid and Invalid Setup Examples

mini-Dow (YM), and the E-mini NASDAQ (NQ), but the preferred contract for volatility is the mini Russell (TF). At $100 per point, any successful breakout play can account for nearly half or more of a reasonable five-point goal for the 1st Frame session. See Section Four for further discussion of trade management. More examples are provided on the book's companion website. Directions to this website can be found in Appendix A.

■ ORB Pennant

The second most successful ORB breakout pattern we have observed at ValhallaFutures is the *ORB Pennant*. As familiar as a pennant is to most traders, I believe most traders miss this potential breakout pattern for two reasons. First, most intraday traders work in the 5-minute bar frame. I admit preferring a longer view than the smaller 1-minute frame myself, but utilize the less commonly used 3-minute bars for that. But for these early breakout patterns, the 1-minute frame is a must. Secondly, the concept of a pennant must be reduced to its simplest components. As the 3-Bar pattern is actually the gesture of a flag pattern reduced to its most basic parts, the ORB Pennant must be reduced to no more than a mere implication. It's like looking at a painting devoid of signature and still recognizing it as that of Joan Miró or Pablo Picasso. The smallest characteristic gesture is indicative of the larger identity's whole. So it is with the power of the market's opening action. Sometimes, a much larger pattern whole is implicated by the smallest identifying gesture. And the implication in potential trend of this characteristic gesture can be nuclear in outcome.

For the ORB Pennant, we look for the first higher low to turn back up and yet fail to make either a higher high or matching high. Instead, it then makes a lower high, and turns yet back inward again. Each of these two turns should be signaled by a change in the candle color to its opposite trend direction, but sometimes a simple Doji indicates the turn back toward the center of the pennant is in place. With the market thus facing two failure attempts at each end to make a new price extreme in either direction, we bracket both the current high and low and enter a pair of trigger positions by means of opposing stop-entry orders, regardless which way the action then goes. Consider that trend has compressed just at the moment where the whole day's expansion is yet ahead; that price has compressed near the ORB, and is nuclear in implication. By breaking out after such a setup, that initial small compression can lead to a chain reaction, sometimes trending thereafter for the entire day. After that, the trade's success, like that of the 3-Bar ORB, is a matter of contract management. See Figure 2.4 from May 31, 2013.

FIGURE 2.4 ORB Pennant Setup and Breakout

Beginner's note: Despite the temptation to bracket the *trend lines* of the pennant with your buy/sell stop orders for a tighter entry price than accomplished by bracketing the high and low of the pennant itself, in most cases, like the one above, it is wisest to bracket your entry orders a tick or two above and below the whole pennant. But when the pennant itself is larger, and is sitting above or below the ORB when it completes, as in Figure 2.5, from June 13, 2013, the bracket can either be entered beyond the high or low of the day, or shifted to just outside the trend lines themselves.

The direction of the breakout can often surprise traders. I remember being confident the one in Figure 2.5 was going to break out to the upside.

FIGURE 2.5 Variation of an ORB Pennant Setup

For more examples of the ORB Pennant, see the book's companion website, with instructions in Appendix A.

■ ORB Matched Highs/Lows

Sometimes price tries but fails to break below or above the initial Opening Range, or a high or low it establishes nearby. If it attempts but fails with at least two, 1-minute bars that have exact matching prices to an initial price extreme at or just beyond the ORB, then chances are good that it will succeed in a breakout out in the opposite direction. Watch for this to set up quickly in the 1-minute time frame, and quickly enter with a stop order at the opposite end of the matching priced bars for a breakout entry to the opposing direction. See Figure 2.6 from May 20, 2013.

This potential pair of matching lows or highs does not have to be the first two 1-minute bars of the day, or be exactly at the Opening Range price limit itself. In fact, it usually isn't. But this pattern setup should be fairly close

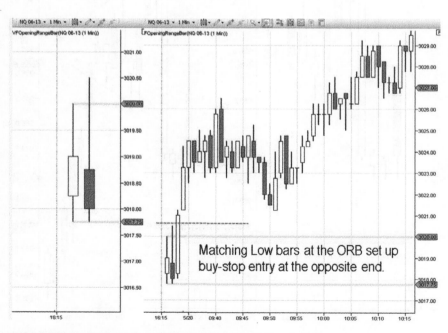

FIGURE 2.6 ORB Matched Lows, Setup and Breakout

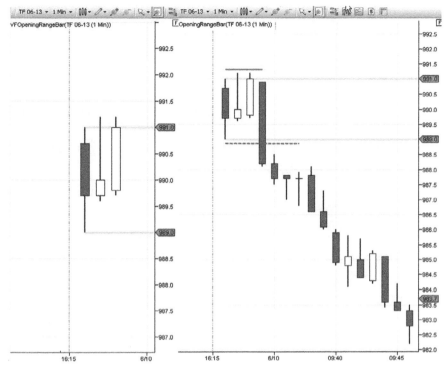

FIGURE 2.7   Matched Highs ORB Setup and Breakdown

to the range limit price, and occur within a few minutes after the actual opening to contain the potential of that nuclear affect contained in the kernel of the ORB, as in Figure 2.7 from June 10, 2013.

For more examples of the Matched ORB Highs/Lows, see the book's companion website, with instructions in Appendix A.

■ Summary

Later chapters will demonstrate that the outcome to the first trend direction of the day is usually a reversal to an even greater trend in the opposite direction. Therefore, trade management does not favor the assumption that any of these initial ORB breakout plays will lead to a Persistent Trend Day in the direction of this initial breakout. Capturing an entire day's trend from one of these breakout plays has far more to do with sufficient contract quantity, enabling position management of a *runner*, than it does with some accurate presage of the day's outcome. See Part Two for more on the Day Model Pattern called Persistent Trend.

■ Notes

1. Toby Crabel, *Day Trading with Short Term Price Patterns and Opening Range Breakout* (Greenville, SC: Trader's Press, 1990).
2. Larry Williams, *Long-Term Secrets to Short-Term Trading* (New York: John Wiley & Sons, 1991).

CHAPTER 3

Pivot / Exhaustion Grid

The alternative title for this chapter might have been the more expected "Support and Resistance Levels." Many traders and methodology vendors rely heavily on the price levels they place above and below the current market each day before the Open. "Watch this key number," one will say. Or, "This number is a *must-hold*." I've even heard chat room vendors of more questionable repute claim they can predict the high or low each day in advance, adding, "We never guess." Drawn in by such claims, many a beginner trader then falsely assumes that knowing tomorrow's high or low in advance is actually the key to successful trading.

But this is simply not the case. In truth, an intraday day trader is only trying to capture a part of some of the many swings the volatile index futures make each day on their eventual journey to the day's destined high or low. An analyst's focus on some exact high or low only betrays his dangerous personal emphasis on being right. And the fundamental wisdom of all truly successful trading has nothing to do with being right. It has everything to do with executing entries when completed technical models appear at the right edge of one's video screen, whether some supposedly magic number has been reached yet or not.

The object of trading is to make a consistent profit. Using only numbers as decision criteria will never achieve this. Price levels of fairly precise support and resistance must be combined with waning momentum signals, completed pattern structure, and time of day to execute profitable trades. Confluence is the key. As for the element of tracking price levels, I have been forced to throw out many methods of acquiring support and resistance that just didn't make a consistent contribution. To that goal I, like a floor trader, have learned to haunt those cherished price levels that dared not be broken, contrary to predicted consequence, for some of the best trading opportunities offered each day. Breaking sacred support and resistance numbers usually runs stop-loss orders, and produces just the exhaustion to trend so often ideal for entry in the opposite direction.

Generally, support and resistance methods fall into one or the other of two categories. The first method derives its potential price levels directly from bar chart formations and pricing. The other depends on mathematical algorithms based on highs, lows, and closes. As we move toward constructing a completed support/resistance grid in this chapter, individual color codes will be assigned to differentiate exhaustion from support/resistance. An exhaustion spike tends to trade through an identified price level, and thus deserves a separate trade management strategy and frame of mind when entering. A simple mnemonic device is employed to pick colors so that all the line plots of the grid are easy to associate with their distinct identities far out into the chart's future, should price return there sometime in the coming hours, days, or weeks, but then devoid of reference as to their source.

■ ORB Kilroy

The Opening Range Bar (ORB) concept was introduced in the previous chapter, and with it a number of trade models that can help identify potential early breakouts from the ORB into an initial trend of the day. But unlike other levels of support, resistance, and exhaustion that are only used once for potential trade entry considerations, the Opening Range is carried forward throughout the entire day and can serve as effectively as an important price level long after the 1st Frame is over. In fact, the ORB actually adds to its effectiveness the longer price has been away from it, but only within the day of origination. The ORB bracket plot is not carried over into the next day, where a fresh Opening Range will be under consideration.

Generally, when price returns to the nearby side of the Opening Range after being away from it for any period of time, it provides resistance. As price returns to this level in the 1st Frame of the day, it is usually the nearby side of the range itself that stops price and is considered resistance, if being approached from below, and support if being approached from above. But when price is returning to this range later in the day, especially in the heat of a fast-paced midday correction, it's the far side of the Opening Range that often comes into play as exhaustion to the pullback. In such corrections, price will often just clip the far side of the ORB enough to run stops that end-of-day swing traders were protecting themselves with, only to then turn right back into the original trend it had just come from. This is especially annoying to such end-of-day traders and can be the source of that oft-quoted, but paranoid and erroneous remark, "They knew where my stops were. They always come to get me."

So powerful is this final exhaustion concept, with price just poking through the far side of the ORB to finish a deep correction to the day's trend, that we give it a folksy name that the intraday swing traders can better identify and include it in concept models for entry and trade exits. "Kilroy was here" was a graffiti remark sometimes left by World War II solders as they marked passage through towns in Europe along the moving front. In truth, its origin is a bit of bathroom humor from the U.S. Midwest, where the image of a cartoon character named Kilroy was drawn to mark an outhouse toilette door, a.k.a. Kilroy's Castle. Apparently this cute little guy never got any more than his nose and eyes and finger tips above the wall of the outhouse, either to let you know his "Castle" was already occupied, or to warn you that Kilroy might be popping up to have a peek in.

Just so does price often just spike through at the far end of the Opening Range, getting no more than a brief glimpse of air before reversing back into trend, against the direction that delivered it, as if exhausted by the effort. The important thing here to remember is that it's *the trip* back from the far distance of the original trend that finally culminates in exhaustion breaking through the Opening Range. Had the journey instead started nearby and not had so far to travel back from the extremes of the previous trend, there would be too little with which to express exhaustion. (See Figure 3.1.)

So powerful is the concept of the ORB as support/resistance, that once committed to one side, price can be very reluctant to visit the opposite. Consider that the pair of charts in Figure 3.2 actually came from the action of the very same day, March 20, 2013; the TF contract being unable to trade below the ORB, while the YM was unable to successfully trade above it. (Remember, by our definition, price has not left the Opening Range unless both the high and low of the bar in question has actually traded beyond the range. Just probing through it does not qualify.)

FIGURE 3.1 The Kilroy Exhausts the Trend Correction

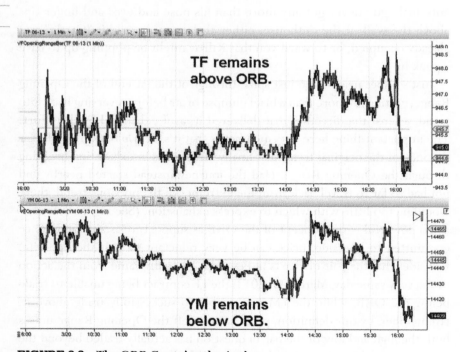

FIGURE 3.2 The ORB Contains the Action

■ Break-Away Pivots: The Pivot Ledge[1]

The *Break-away Pivot*™ is not an algorithm, and it falls into the first category of being derived directly from the bar charts themselves. A particular price pattern must be formed in order for a horizontal line plot to be constructed as an indicator for future support or resistance. Swing points in bar charts are normally thought of as previous highs and lows where short-term reversals have occurred. But a Break-away Pivot does not occur at a nearby high or low. It occurs at the shoulder of the pattern formation where a sudden price movement is steeply accelerated. In the wake of this break-away pattern, a ledge is left behind that will be the basis of significant future support/resistance. The *Pivot Ledge*™ defines the focal point of a Break-away Pivot where future support/resistance will be the most insurmountable should price return there. The Pivot Ledge is often *death* to the current trend, so its plot is styled in a *black*, dash-dotted line. The concept is easier to understand visually than in words. (See Figures 3.3 and 3.4.)

It was two days before the ES contract had the opportunity to test that Ledge in Figure 3.4 for support, whereupon it was met with very sharp price rejection. Studies of this concept on the histories of cash indices

FIGURE 3.3 Pivot Ledge Plotted

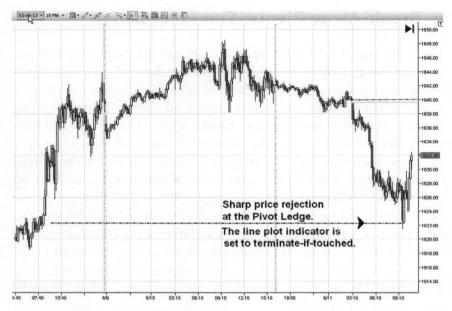

Sharp price rejection
at the Pivot Ledge.
The line plot indicator is
set to terminate-if-touched.

FIGURE 3.4 Pivot Ledge Retested

demonstrate this concept can be carried forward for years and years and still meet the same result when price returns to an earlier Pivot Ledge for the first time. Break-away Pivots can be found on any chart. It just takes a little practice. Note the one that was created on the way back down from the same price data period, in the chart of Figure 3.4. Think of a bear Pivot Ledge like the edge of waterfall, seemingly calm until it reaches the steep drop-off where a violent acceleration ensues.

■ The Break-Away Lap

When price breaks away sharply from one of these shoulder formations in the lower time frames of intraday charts, it often leaves the tiniest lapse in price behind as a telltale mark, so-named a Lap. A Lap is a missing tick between the close of one bar and opening of another, which does not close immediately. In thinner markets or in the daily frame, such a *Break-away Lap*™ may actually leave a true gap, which is a missing tick between the actual high and low of any two adjacent bars, leaving a little "air" in between them. A Lap leaves no air. The Lap phenomenon can happen sporadically throughout the day, as in Figure 3.5. In the extremely liquid ES contract,

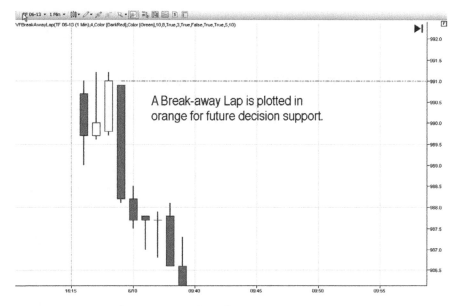

FIGURE 3.5 Break-Away Lap Plotted

an intraday Lap is seldom created at all, but appears quite commonly in the thinner YM, NQ, and TF contracts.

A red dashed line indicator is reserved for a true gap in the daily frame bars, plotted from a previous Y-Close. A Lap is less significant, and so it is plotted in orange. (See the Wiley companion website for a colorized version of Figure 3.5.) Since this line might be projected out onto the charts for many days into the future, it's important to know what that line means should price return to it when considering a trade decision. Since these small laps are not easily noticed, an indicator is programmed to plot them automatically, label the price and date from which they occur, and terminate them when retested, as in Figure 3.6.

(Aside: If these data lapses are fairly hard to see, it begs the question, why does the market seem to know where they are, return to them for retest, and react to them thereafter? I believe this is a clear clue to the theory on which much of this book and nearly all of my own trading success is based; that there is, in fact, an internal structure to the market that relies on hidden principles of mass behavior.)

Sometimes a Break-away Lap will occur near the Pivot Ledge of the break-away pattern, sometimes not. Sometimes a Lap will be created without this shoulder formation, simply at a place where price accelerated suddenly.

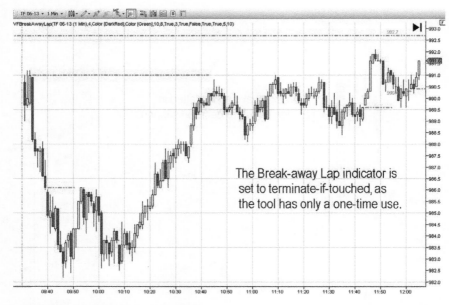

FIGURE 3.6 Break-Away Laps Retested

The chart in Figure 3.6 is a continuation in time from that depicted in the charts for Figures 3.4 and 3.5, from the second week of June 2013. Leaving an untested Pivot Ledge or Break-away Lap behind is like *unfinished business* for the market, as if calling it back before further business can be conducted. Most traders are well aware of this phenomenon of gap closure in the daily frame, but fewer take advantage of it for intraday trading of entries and exits, and fewer still seem to be aware that it is really not the open Lap that's the real issue at all. Instead, it's the violent break and Pivot Ledge that seem to call the market back to be touched there again. (See Figure 3.7.)

The question is often asked in webinars whether a trade can be initiated right when a Break-away Pivot begins. Unfortunately, this usually happens too quickly to be a useful tool for the beginning of a position. And besides, many Laps are quickly closed before they gain the stature that only time and distance from origin can give them.

Now take another closer look at the sequence of charts in Figures 3.3, 3.4, and 3.7. It tells a familiar story of how chart patterns are built over time, especially in the areas where price is beginning to consolidate, something it does more than 80 percent of the time. Even if you don't have the software to auto-draw them, it only takes a bit of practice to note where

Pivot Ledge
from previous day

FIGURE 3.7 Open Break-Away Lap as "Unfinished Business"

Break-away Pivots exist, and plot them by hand. In the chart of Figure 3.7, another Pivot Ledge appeared and had the same effect on price. The line plot for this Ledge was deleted from the chart intentionally as a sort of practice lesson. Take a moment to find where it was created, and how price reacted when returning to it a short time later, at around 14:40 (2:40 P.M.) ET. An intraday trader might only have to catch a single ride from one Pivot Ledge to another to earn that day's profit goal.

In summary, the Pivot Ledge leaves unfinished business on the charts, as if calling price back to test that level. But, keep in mind that no market will remain trapped between these support and resistance numbers for long before breaking free into the trend of the larger time frame.

■ Previous Highs and Lows

Most traders keep yesterday's high, low, and closing price levels marked on the chart when considering today's trades. But how are these used? I find most traders put too much credence to the oft-quoted axiom that a higher high is a sign of an uptrend, a new lower low for a downtrend. The action of the index futures seems almost geared to confuse the majority, and I find that for intraday positioning, the opposite might be said to be true. Just about the time yesterday's low—so-named the Y-Low—has been broken by falling price, the trend is ready to turn and go up. Even if the market is destined to extend further down or up later in the day, this initial break of the Y-Low or Y-High, especially when there is little or no follow-through, is almost sure to get the opposite trend reaction started.

"They knew where my stop was hiding. They can see the book. They came and got me," or so the less experienced trader is prone to say after being taken out of his position just beyond a current high or low. Of course, this is nonsense. Or more correctly, everyone knows the stops are placed just beyond the lows and highs. Who needs "the book" to know that? Floor traders haunt these places. Where else would they be? But the inexperienced trader believes that somewhere "they" are huddled in personal conspiracy to attack his hidden stop-loss orders.

So, unlike traders who hold to the belief that some low or high must hold for a trend to be secure, these daily highs and lows, and their counterparts the night session highs and lows, can be seen as levels of exhaustion. And when added to a confluence of other technical phenomena appearing at the same time, the break of an existing high or low can be an excellent entry point, entering a position just where others are being stopped out.

One feature of our larger Pivot/Exhaustion Grid extends these lines into the future indefinitely until hit or crossed. And when some days have passed, and the source of that line plot can no longer be seen, it is important as a potential element of trade strategy to know whether the line plot in question was a Y-High or Y-Low, or an overnight high or low, sometimes referred to as the Globex High or Low, which uses *all-session data*. To facilitate the recognition of lines that appear again within the current daily range from some day weeks ago, we can use a simple mnemonic memory scheme for color coding and line style. *The sky above us is light blue*, so we color code all previous highs in cyan, using a heavier dash style for the former daily highs, and a *thin line for the less important* overnight highs. The *sea below us is dark blue*, so we color lows accordingly. A monthly or weekly low is far more important than a mere daily low or overnight low. So we program our indicator to carry the date that pivot was created into part of the label that accompanies the line. All these lines are plotted forward in time indefinitely until price meets or exceeds them in the *day-only session*. Our indicator is set to *Terminate-if-Touched*.[2] So once price meets them, the plot carries no further, so as to keep the screen uncluttered of price levels no longer of concern.

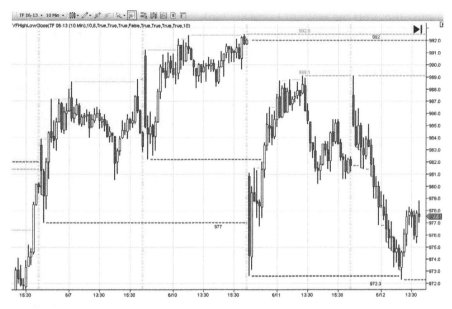

FIGURE 3.8 Price Breaks Y-Lows

There are four days' worth of 10-minute bars in the chart example in Figure 3.8: An entire Friday, Monday, Tuesday, and part of Wednesday can be seen from June 7 through June 12, 2013. The vertical yellow lines denote session breaks. Both the session break and the ORB are plotted in yellow as a mnemonic memory device. *The day begins with sunshine yellow.* (For a colorized version, see the Wiley companion website.) Note the action following the break of previous days' Y-Lows. It would give an intraday trader little consolation against continual stop-loss executions to note that eventually price was below all these lows if he used his axiom of "a downtrend = lower lows" to justify a short entry every time one broke. The price reaction at those breaks was bullish, not bearish. Although he can certainly claim he was right about the trend eventually, "they" took all his money in the meantime. A great deal of the time, lows actually have to be taken out before the market gathers enough energy to go back making higher highs. **Be wary of commonly accepted trading axioms.** And remember the wisdom of Heraclitus: "Even the scholar most in repute knows only what is reputed, and holds fast to just that."

I once watched a video from a notoriously successful Internet vendor that was distributed to their nonmembers to be helpful and to promote their growing membership. In it, the vendor suggested as a trade entry setup to short the break of the Globex Low when-if price should break that level during the morning session. I actually look for this same event almost every day, but for a trade in the opposite direction. It should be noted that the market has a much easier time of breaking and staying below a Y-Low if it doesn't have to travel far to get to it. It's often *the trip* that wears the market out, and thus meets exhaustion when a low or high is finally taken. These are the best price extremes to fade with countertrend trades, and methodical tracking-until-touched of all the previous Y-High and Y-Low line plots is essential for the intraday trader. But Traders take note: Once taken out and counter trend reactions have set in, lows and highs are, indeed, often excellent levels for breakout trades, and had that notoriously successful vendor explained that more fully, that advice would have been far less damaging to their membership.

■ Previous Closing Prices: The Gap

The same tracking issue is important for all the Y-Closes from day-only session data charts, sometimes called gap-charts. But rather than thinking in terms of exhaustion at the Y-Close, a Gap-Close is better thought of as support or resistance, with reasonable expectations of price rejection once accomplished. As per other numbers on our grid, opening right near the Y-Close will provide little or no reaction when price crosses it. It's the trip getting there that usually makes it significant. For the mnemonic memory device, we use a heavy red-dash plot for the Y-Close line. *A red traffic stop sign is placed at the end of each road.*

In recent years, a large number of vendors have offered the Gap-Close as a trader's play in their education products. Their basic strategy is to take a position sometime after the Open, back in the direction of the gap itself, with an eye to following price back to that previous day's Close (i.e., the Gap-Close). This trade seems to work just enough to keep traders coming back. But the stats are not as encouraging as promoted. For instance, just using a review of the June 2013 E-mini Russell futures (TF) contract at the time of this book, there were about 39 gaps in the TF of at least 2 points or more over the 90-day period. Of those 39 gaps only 6 closed within the first trend of the day. About 9 took the entire day and often only after price moved to expand the gap further first, sometimes referred to as "Gap-n-Go." Some 11 did not close until two days later, and some 13 did not close until three days or more, with about 5 of those not closing for nearly 30 days, or still pending.

Most futures traders cannot tolerate a wide enough stop-loss risk to survive even one day as price works against their position. But for argument's sake, allowing for those traders who did hold their TF Gap-Close positions all day during the period noted above, just 15 of those 39 Gap-Close trades made a profit on the day of occurrence, leaving 24 where a Gap-n-Go position would have done much better.

Different results, however, could be accomplished from considering this trade from the other end of the gap altogether. During that same period, using the same TF contract, price bounced *off* the gap and reversed when it finally did close, regardless of how many days or hours it took to return there, 21 of the 39 times within a point or so of contact. Some 6 more of those 39 Gap-Closes provided at least enough profit for partial exit of a multi-contract reversal position to move the stop-loss on the remainder to net break-even risk. Only 8 of the total 39 failed to reverse at all, and a loss from entering those as reversals would presume a trader would not wait at least the length of a 1-minute bar to see if, in fact, price would hold at the Y-Close, and then turn back toward the Open.

So here's a different suggestion regarding this Gap-Close trade concept: Take early, intraday positions in futures contracts using methods independent of the existence of any opening gap. Ignore it. And instead, consider using the gap closing itself, whenever that technical event finally does occur, as a possible entry point back in the original gap direction, with other trade model entry filters considered. Think of the Y-Close as but another number in a support and resistance grid of numbers, albeit of greater significance than some others. Yes, it's true that gaps usually do close, but the more consistent trade entry apparently is at the point of closure, back in the direction of the original opening gap, rather than in any position taken in expectation that the gap will close quickly.

Appendix G further demonstrates how affective trade entry at gap closure can be as compared to other entry identification methods, such as Fibonacci.

■ Tick Bar Laps

Using tick bars instead of time bars in charting is like looking at the market under a microscope. I always hesitate to show these tricks to students who haven't yet completed trade model setups in their trade plans lest they be tempted to try trading from tick bars to initiate trade ideas. Internet trading platforms are like video games and slot machines. It's so tempting to just click-and-send orders from a price ladder and see the results of real money transferring into your account so immediately. The problem is, that money leaves just as quickly. **Trade models must come from a confluence of**

disparate indicators arriving simultaneously in price and time. And a trade plan is designed to impose discipline over the activity of trade entry and exit. But once a trade model's criteria has appeared at the right edge of one's video screen, examining price action in close-up can improve profits tremendously by means of better timed priced fills—as long as a trade model's price target has actually arrived first. This can't be stressed enough.

Following is an anatomy of a trade that began in the 3-minute bars as the Midday Frame was coming to an end. The rally off the lows around 1:30 P.M. was the biggest reversal seen all day in a day of continual selling. The reversal was dramatic enough to have left two Pivot Ledges in its wake. According to my own trade plan, there was not a completed trade model to identify that reversal as a low until it was well past. But that didn't stop me from monitoring the ensuing action for a pullback. The chart below in Figure 3.9 shows how the 3-minute bars reacted when the nearer of those two Ledges was reached.

In the tick bar chart for the same time period, Figure 3.10, a Lap was present at that higher Pivot Ledge that was not visible in the 3-bar chart frame in Figure 3.9. Study the chart.

On the way down to closing that Lap at the higher of the two Pivot Ledges, another Tick Bar Lap was left open on the trip down, lending itself as fresh, unfinished business for an eventual trip back up.

FIGURE 3.9 Trade Anatomy in 3-Minute Bars

FIGURE 3.10 A View of 6-Tick Bars as a "Microscope" of the 1-Minute Bars in Figure 3.9

Using the upper Tick Bar Lap as a target for taking a long at that Pivot Ledge would have left money on the table should the budding bull trend continue to develop. But that's not the point. The mini Russell typically moves in two- to three-point spurts before pausing or pulling back in its trends. At $100 per point, it only takes capturing a couple of these swings to reach a modest profit goal per frame for an individual trader. And a multiple contract management system can allow for a runner to be held at a break-even or near break-even stop-loss. Be the Trader. The Trader doesn't predict. He positions.

■ Dynamic Exhaustion Levels: The EMAs

A moving average is nothing more than a plot of average prices over some selected look-back period. The exponential moving average is simply a modification to the formula. Some methods employ moving averages as signal generators, using the cross of one over the other as an indicator of trend change. Those EMAs tend to use shorter look-back periods in order to reduce the lag effect of the signal. But with longer look-back periods, these same lines can be effective levels of short-term exhaustion as price culminates in short-term price spikes. When used in conjunction with 1-minute price bars, the 200 and

89 period EMA's plot excellent levels of exhaustion and move dynamically throughout the day as price trend proceeds.

These two EMAs are not used as a crossover signal system, but they do exhibit important trend information. The relationship between price bars and these EMAs becomes repetitive and can contribute to trade entry models with specific criteria. A whole set of these behaviorisms has been reserved for a later chapter. As for its contribution to the Pivot/Exhaustion Grid, these two EMAs are color coded in green. The memory device is to compare them to *foliage:* for the 200EMA, *dark green*, as it *older and slower*, and for the 89EMA, *light green*, as it better reflects the *newer and faster* price action. See Part Three, Chapter 15 ("EMA Pattern Concepts") for how these dynamic support/resistance lines contribute to specific trade-entry models.

The 1-minute time bars have been used in this section regarding concepts like the ORB and Pivot Ledge and Break-away Lap in order to view the precision with which they are created. However, tremendous decision support can be garnered from the larger time frames as well. In the 60-minute frame, exponential moving averages from the 19 to the 26 look-back period will appear to contain price when trending well, and serve as a midpoint to action in a trading range, as in Figure 3.11.

FIGURE 3.11 TF 60-Minute, Day-Session Bars with a 21 Period EMA

FIGURE 3.12 60-Minute Frame MAs Viewed from within 1-Minute Bars

Remembering to flip back and forth between such larger time frames at critical moments of trade decision seldom happens for the busy intraday trader. So in order to bring this decision support into view, those 60-minute EMAs can be converted to a 1300-period EMA for the 1-minute bars. I add to this a 1300 Simple Moving Average (SMA), which creates a small band or zone of support/resistance for this indicator in the 1-minute bars. With an acknowledgment of the variation in volatility among our four contracts, ES, YM, NQ, and TF, the look-back numbers 1140 and 1560 can also be tested. To do so, open 60-minute, day-only session charts for each contract. Then examine 19, 21, and 26EMAs for each in this larger frame. You're looking for an EMA that appears to just guide price along when trending well, and as a midpoint to price action when its working out a range. Those three 60-minute choices correspond to 1140, 1300, and 1560EMAs in the 1-minute bars. Figure 3.12 displays the translation of the 21-period EMA from the 60-minute frame to the 1-minute bars by means of the 1300EMA, *in light brown for faster and newer*, and the 1300SMA, *in dark brown for older and slower*. (See the Wiley companion website for a colorized version.)

■ Floor Trader's Pivot Points

Floor trader's pivots are *Old School*, but experience keeps them in the mix of tools for support/resistance. There has always been a question of whether they tend to work because everyone knows of and anticipates them, or because they reflect something inherent to internal structure projected from yesterday's range into today's. Some analysts like to use the first hour to create another set of pivots and project those out into the remainder of the day. If one's emphasis for swings is the 1st Frame of the day, this technique is of less interest.

Of notable concern to many traders who attempt to use these numbers is the apparent difference in the output for the pivot indicator between one charting software and another. It's very typical in chat rooms for two traders quoting the *Daily Pivot Point* to have different numbers. If the Daily Pivot (DP) number is different, the set of corresponding support and resistance numbers, labeled *S1*, *S2*, *S3*, *R1*, *R2*, and *R3* will show even greater discrepancies because the derivative formula exaggerates the spread.

First, let's assume they are using the same formula, although variations in this formula now abound. I still find the traditional formula the most consistent: the DP = the Y-High + the Y-Low + the Y-Close / 3. Newer formulas trying to incorporate the Opening gap will add today's Open and then divide by 4. This sounds logical, but as we all know, the market isn't. I don't find these newer versions make the tool more useful or accurate for potential turns at these newer projected levels of support/resistance. This observation tends to give credence to the theory that pivot points work because everyone uses them, and thus are anticipated by traders.

The real issue in discrepancies between users for the output set is the data vendor, not the charting-software package. The data vendor eSignal®[3] includes something called Settlement Close for the final price of a futures contract within its data stream, which is often slightly different than the last tick traded at 4:15 P.M. ET. Settlement Close is a tradition in the physical commodity futures because some of those instruments don't always have a final tick at the closing bell. Instead, they report a Close extrapolated between the last bid/offer. Furthermore, eSignal issues the Y-High and Y-Low from the all-session daily bar range, rather than the day-only session. Often the day's session is extended dramatically in the evening hours while European sources publish their news and economic events. Naturally, a calculation based on this range instead of the day-only session range would produce a different set of pivot point numbers. Another popular data vendor, CQG®[4] does not use the all-session daily bar to extrapolate the High,

Low, and Close, and thus produces a different set of numbers for the Floor Trader's Pivot Point indicator than does eSignal.

The response I've heard from many traders on this subject is that since they only trade the day session, they only want to use that range to project potential turning points for tomorrow's action. Logical, but again, the market is not. Besides, what happens in the evening session is talked about all morning and the entire trading community is aware of the night's business news well before the NYSE rings its opening bell. But that's not really the point either. What works more consistently to identify real turning points is clearly the more desirable, and in my experience, those calculations reflecting truer real-time price pivots are derived from using the daily all-session price range bars for this indicator.

In summary, the recommended technique is to take the pivots from the all-session price range and then apply it to a day-only session chart for the Pivot Grid. If more convenient, the daily published pivots at the website MyPivots.com are derived using all-session price bars.

■ Fibonacci Targets

One of the most widely used methods now to create a support and resistance grid is the Fibonacci retracement and extension tool set. I have tested and used such tools extensively, and I have studied the use of these tools by well-known analysts and vendors such as Robert Miner's Dynamic Traders[5] and Robert Prechter's Elliott Wave International.[6] My own experience as a trader shows that Fibonacci is the ideal tool for vendors to give seminars and sell education tools. When demonstrating trade entries, a Fibonacci number is always nearby. When you consider overlapping both a retracement and an extension grid, and use daily and weekly ranges from both directions to do so, you create so many lines on the page that every important turn is bound to be near at least one of them. All a vendor needs do is cherry-pick which one worked for some specific case, and use that in the demonstration. Better yet, turning sloppiness to apparent advantage, software can be designed to identify places where Fibonacci extension and retracement lines from various time frames bunch up the most in concentration, and target those areas for entries and exits.

It's become almost politically incorrect to even question such sacred science. But my conclusions are not positive. Many market turns may have a Fibonacci number nearby, but most Fibonacci numbers do not produce market turns. In fact, most don't even produce reactions.

I no longer rely on Fibonacci as an element to trade entry models, but must acknowledge, however, that there is indeed an internal structure to market pattern and price fulfillment that is repetitive in nature, and believe using Fibonacci to target exits instead of entries can be of tremendous value. One such trend targeting method we call the *Inverse 78.6% Projection Rule.* Simply stated, that rule targets the excursion of a budding trend to an additional 78.6 percent of further distance as measured from the Ledge of a sharp Break-away Pivot, when assumed to have been formed 21.4 percent away from the nearby reversal extreme of the nearby high or low. See Figure 3.13.

Take note of the chart in Figure 3.13 for later reference. This chart selection is reused in Chapter 17, Figure 17.11, to display further trend progress,

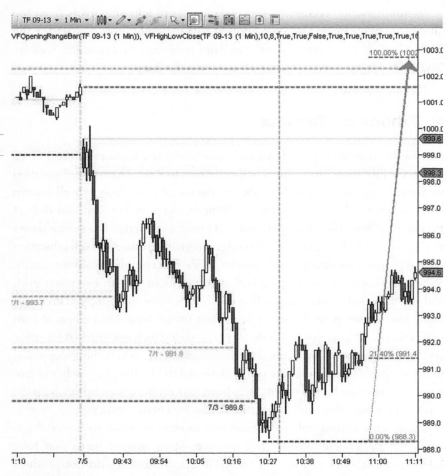

FIGURE 3.13 A Pivot Ledge 21.4 Percent of the Way to Target

with a purpose of building the story of confluence toward a true Trade Entry Model. (Colorized versions are available on the Wiley companion website.)

For a specific example of comparison between more traditional Fibonacci methods and those used from our Grid to derive support/resistance numbers, see Appendix G.

■ Measured Move Targets

Targets are integral tools to any serious support and resistance grid. As discussed, the Pivot Ledge itself can serve as *unfinished business*, calling the market back, as if to the target of the next reversal. Chart pattern breakouts also create trend targets, and are integral to keeping our Pivot/Exhaustion Grid up-to-date. The Symmetrical Triangle leaves a horizontal line plot at its apex for future support/resistance and also targets a breakout excursion of equal distance to that of its open jaw; the Head-n-Shoulders breakout targets an excursion distance equal to the price traversed from the extreme tip of the head to the broken neckline; the Midday Channel leaves behind a centerline plot that serves the same purpose as the apex of a triangle for support/resistance, from which an excursion target can be measured as equidistant from the channel's opposite trend extreme to the formation of its centerline; and the Rising/Declining Diagonal Wedge measures the base origin of the pattern itself as a target to the impending reversal. All four of these will be discussed in Part Three, "Repetitive Chart Patterns."

■ Market Profile

Few methodologies have given birth to more vendor services than the method of determining support and resistance called Market Profile®.[7] (See Figure 3.14.)

Market Profile calculates the price most often crossed throughout the day, and/or the price point that generated the most total volume, and labels this price as the Point of Control (POC). From there a bell curve with two, bracketing 75-percent lines creates a Value Area for considering trades.

Perhaps there are many traders who use this tool effectively every day. The problem I found was that the method did not contribute effectively to precise trade-setup-model specifics. Except for using the Point of Control itself as a price level of support/resistance, the rest of the tool's information seems soft, approximate, and only vaguely effective as decision support. A

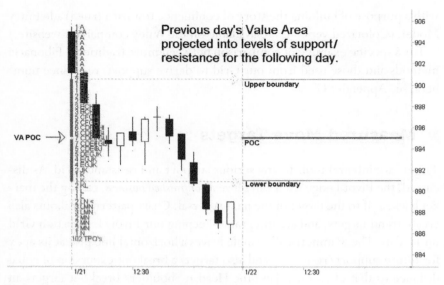

FIGURE 3.14 Value Area and Point of Control

Trade Plan can't survive on tendencies. Tendencies lead to tape reading and tape reading leads to intuition. A Trade Plan can accommodate no intuition. I'm sure Pete Steidlmayer,[8] author of the concept, would sincerely disagree, as would hundreds of his protégés. I defer to their expertise on the subject for their own trading, and to the reader for further investigation and conclusions of his or her own.

The Point of Control (POC), at the very least, can make a valuable addition to your support/resistance grid. Depending on the charting-software package you use, you may or may not have Market Profile included as an indicator. If not, Volume-at-Price is a good approximation, as the price that created the most volume is often near or the same as the price that received the most separate trade hits. But if there is no substitute in your charting software for Market Profile, you can still get the daily POC from a website called MyPivots.com, at least at the time of this book's publication, and transfer it to your own charts each day by hand.

■ Trend Lines

Traders often ignore the most powerful way to use trend lines because traders dwell solely in the frame they are trading. Day traders are particularly guilty of this. They draw lots of local trend lines, but forget to reach back into the larger time frames for trend line plots. Try using the 15-, 45-, and/ or 60-minute trends from the all-session format. Don't think about it too much. Just eyeball the connecting lows and highs. Sometimes a trend will break down only to be recaptured later. Sometimes the simplest visuals can be the most significant message for trading. Carry your artwork back into the lower time frames of the day-only session data. Use a unique line plot style to tie its identity to that of the larger time frame from which it originated, and to differentiate it from trend lines you're drawing in the lower frame. The whole point of creating a Pivot/Exhaustion Grid is to identify relationships in pattern and price and carry them out into subsequent daily action as it unfolds among other disparate, technical tools. (See Figure 3.15.)

Having had the chart lines that were created in the 60-minute, all-session frame, as seen in Figure 3.15, plotted into the smaller time-frame bars where the intraday trader operates could have clearly signaled the high and low resistance levels at some three dozen contact points over the three-month period in view at the time of this book's writing. That is no small thing when looking for the likeliest pivots where the market might turn.

The mistake many traders make is not using all-session data when prescribing trend lines in the larger time frames for day-only session trade entry considerations. Compare the all-session, 60-minute TF chart in Figure 3.15 again to the earlier 60-minute, day-only session TF chart in Figure 3.11.

FIGURE 3.15 **Trend Lines from an All-Session, 60-Minute TF Chart**

The day-only data is sometimes called a Gap Chart, and is good for viewing the unfinished business of open gaps. But for drawing trend lines, use all-session data.

And notice how trend lines and channels in Figure 3.15 can be recaptured once they've broken down. Peter Brandt has made a lifelong career using this simple technique, among others, in the daily frame for position trading of physical commodity futures and has noted pointedly the negative consequences to his trading from occasionally failing to extend the lines into future time space on his charts.[9] Price tends to return to previously covered ground, and often does so by tracking previously established trend lines.

For intraday trading where exits are modest and targets are only segments of the longer term trends, a trend line originating from the larger frame is an essential number to the day's Pivot/Exhaustion Grid. If your software doesn't automatically carry trend lines drawn within the larger time frame into the smaller frames as scaling is reduced, bring them in by hand. Don't leave home without them.

■ Summary

The Pivot/Exhaustion Grid comprises the Opening Range Bar bracket line pair, intraday high-lows, daily high-lows, overnight high-lows, daily closes, all Pivot Ledges, Break-away Laps, Floor Trader Pivots, specific exponential moving averages, triangle apexes, channel centerlines, Fibonacci and Measured Move targets, Market Profile's Point of Control and trend lines. This horizontal grid is composed from both actual history of price pattern and calculation upon that history. The scheme is then punctuated vertically by the static cycles of Time Frame Transition to complete an underlying grid to future price performance. When combined with the other elements in the following chapters of this book, the arrival of price at future intersections of this grid can be used as the key elements to trade entry models.

■ Notes

1. The terms *Break-away Pivot*, *Pivot Ledge*, *Serial Divergence*, *Serial Sequent*, and some other original terms in this book have pending trademark registration.
2. The ValhallaFutures Indicator Package for NinjaTrader.com includes this as a custom feature preference for certain lines within the Pivot/

TIME FRAME CONCEPTS

Exhaustion Grid indicators (see Appendix C). Other charting software packages might offer similar preferences, or allow custom programming to achieve the same. NinjaCharts is a free download from ValhallaFutures.com.

3. The term *eSignal* is a registered trademark of the eSignal suite of products and a wholly-owned subsidiary of Interactive Data, Bedford, Massachusetts.

4. The abbreviation *CQG* is a registered trademark of the CQG Corporation, Denver, Colorado.

5. Robert C. Miner, *High Probability Trading Strategies: Entry to Exit Tactics for the Forex, Futures, and Stock Markets* (Hoboken, NJ: John Wiley & Sons, 2008).

6. Robert R. Prechter and A. J. Frost, *Elliott Wave Principle* (Gainesville, GA: New Classics Library, 2004).

7. Market Profile® is a registered trademark of the CME Group.

8. J. Peter Steidlmayer, *Steidlmayer on Markets: Trading with Market Profile* (Hoboken, NJ: John Wiley & Sons, 2002).

9. Peter L. Brandt and Bruce Babcock Jr., *Trading Commodity Futures with Classical Chart Patterns* (Sacramento, CA: Advanced Trading Seminars, 1990).

CHAPTER 4

Dough Bar to Die Bar

The concept of the Dough Bar is very simple. Many writers have observed this basic phenomenon: Trends often begin and end with a wide-ranging bar. This bar usually stands out very clearly as the widest range bar among its peers, and as a candlestick pattern, it often forms with very small wicks, or none at all. Coming at the beginning of the day, as with a breakout from the Opening Range Bar (ORB), it can be especially significant.

Coming at the end of the trend, it should be understood that the ending Die Bar is the same trend color as was its initial Dough Bar. That serves an important purpose when trying to time a position exit. In intraday trading, it is usually far more profitable to exit as price is still thrusting in the direction of the trend than waiting out a trailing stop-loss order as the only exit strategy. Since a two- to three-point target is a reasonable expectation when trading something like the mini-Russell, a trailing stop order might give away half or more of that profit in a typical pullback to a trailing stop-loss placement.

The appearance of the Die Bar often comes at the end of one of these intraday swings and offers a greater potential exit opportunity before the market turns back in correction. In other words, a trader should be encouraged in his position when a trend begins itself with the appearance of a Dough Bar, but discouraged about the trend's continued progress when another wide-ranging bar appears after several legs in the trend have transpired.

VFOpeningRangeBar(TF 09-13 (1 Min)), VFHighLowClose(TF 09-13 (1 Min),10,8,True,True,True,False,True,True,True,10)

A Dough Bar ignites the trend.

TF

A Die Bar exhausts the trend.

983.3

982.2

FIGURE 4.1 Dough Bar to Die Bar

When a Dough Bar leaves the ORB, it often reflects the urgency pent up in the market to begin an initial trend for the day. Few traders are looking at 1-minute bars this early in the day. It's the proverbial early bird to the worm that captures Opening Range breakout trades in the smaller frames.

In the chart in Figure 4.1, a second wide-ranging bar appeared after price closed the previous day's gap at the low. Many less-experienced traders might have been encouraged by this bar's appearance as if it indicated a resurgence of the bear trend. But don't be fooled. All the more did this wide bar signal a possible end-of-trend when follow-through action failed to appear shortly thereafter. This is the Die Bar's duty. Along with a possible Dough Bar, it can often bookend the trend. Consider that the information stored in both these signals would have remained invisible to the trader monitoring the action of the 1st Frame with 5-minute bars.

As for anticipating the Dough Bar before it appears by means of an early entry, that's nearly impossible. There may or may not have been a signal to have entered before it began. If there was such an entry signal first, seeing the trend start off with one of these, already having taken the position, is good reassurance that several more waves of profit opportunity will probably follow. But such an early entry might may have been far more luck than skill. The trader faces getting in late to the Dough Bar on most instances, and that is not always so easy in the heat of the action. When reviewing past charts and examining the day in retrospect, it appears so easy to have taken a trade in the direction of the Dough Bar even well after it had occurred because it appeared so early in the trend's eventual destiny. But in real time, at the moment the Dough Bar is forming, a trader can suffer from the feeling that he is chasing the trend and is already too late to get in.

To assuage this anxiety, the appearance of a Dough Bar should be better understood as putting some confirmation into a trend's beginning, and some cushion between the beginning of the trend direction and the risk yet ahead on its way toward a possible target. In the mini-Russell contract, the Dough Bar can often be nearly two points in range, but its appearance usually means there are another two points left or more in the current segment of the trend before a significant correction begins. If the trader will think in terms of capturing his profit goal in such two-point segments, he can be much less uncertain about getting in with a Dough Bar now behind him, paying up with a premium, as it were, for reduction in risk.

Take the example of the chart in Figure 4.2, for instance. Many traders would be *playing the gap* here, using a technique of taking an upside break-out of the ORB after the first 5 or 10 minutes. The Gap-Close play looks so tempting that it builds the trader's psyche with expectation.

All the more difficult would it be then to enter in the opposite direction after the sudden appearance of the Dough Bar, signalling the beginning of an opposing trend against all built-up mental expectations. Eventually a gap got closed, alright. Just not the one our gap traders had their minds set on. See this outcome in Figure 4.3. (A colorized version can be found on the Wiley companion website.)

As the Trader, it's not easy to turn one's rally cap backward and change a mindset. But the Dough Bar does provide a good cushion against the improbability that the surprising new trend direction might reverse yet again, and head back up immediately.

Many intraday swing trends may get started with a Dough Bar or end with a Die Bar, but lots of rallies can end without a Die Bar and begin without a Dough Bar. (See Figure 4.4.)

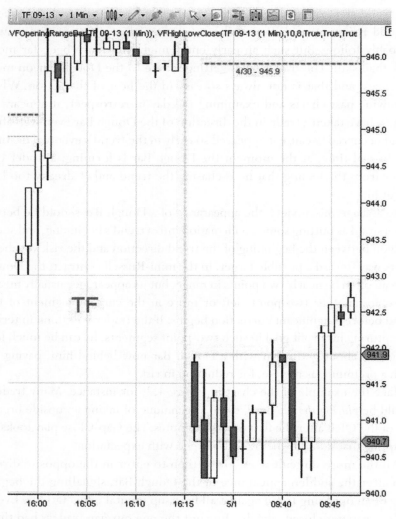

FIGURE 4.2 Trade Anatomy

FIGURE 4.3 Trade Anatomy with Dough and Die Bars

FIGURE 4.4 Dough and Die Bars Not always Present

■ Summary

The Dough Bar–Die Bar bookends can only serve as an assist to an entry model or an exit target. They may contribute to a Trade Entry Model but can't be said to make up one on their own. And waiting to act only after one finally appears may leave the Trader on the sidelines too much of the time. Instead, let it be an additive to the decision support that normally accumulates around the price levels where the market is destined to pivot or break out.

CHAPTER 5

Leadership Divergence

O ne of the most useful tools for trade setups in the 1st Frame of the day is an understanding of leadership and its corollary, divergence. Most traders only focus on the index instrument they trade, and at that, most index traders only trade the E-mini S&P (symbol ES). To borrow again from my mentor Randolph Newman, who is quoted at the start of Part One, "*Everybody* is always wrong." The market by its most fundamental nature is a contrary animal. Advisory services abound that use contrary opinion to call the tops and bottoms of markets. But it goes further: Common axioms for trading mislead traders into dos and don'ts, and cans and can'ts to the point where the most basic of assumptions with which traders now approach the market must be questioned. "Never sell a new high or buy a new low" is one of those axioms that deserve an immediate examination by new traders. And advice about *what* to trade among the main index futures contracts is also worth examining closely.

And just so as to push traders a bit into expanding their watch list to include several index contracts simultaneously, let's examine the assumptions that put the ES contract to the common forefront. "The E-mini S&P 500 contract leads the market." Utter nonsense. And yet I've heard so-called head traders and self-inflated analysts in vendor-based chat rooms make this claim as a given. Seldom does the ES contract lead the Dow Jones 30 (contract symbol YM); almost never does it lead the Nasdaq 100 (symbol NQ); and only very rarely does it ever lead the mini Russell 2000 (symbol TF).

"The ES contract is the most liquid." The ES contract does, indeed, have the highest volume. But high volume liquidity does not always translate to easier entry and exit for the small trader. In fact, the words liquidity and exit are sometimes mutually exclusive. Just try getting out of your ES contract at a two-point target some time and notice how many times it might hit that price before letting you out. "Liquidity" also means significant competition with large-sized orders that stand between you and a fill, whether entry or exit.

Complicating the process of getting a fill at a specific price in the ES is the size of the contract's trading increment. At one-quarter-point increments instead of one-tenth, the ES contract trades like an old clunker automobile. By the time you have decided that you might not get a fill at some particular price, the ES might have pulled away a half or even a full point from the price level of your attempted entry or exit, putting a serious dent in your profit goals for that trade, especially when trying to exit a partial position quickly as a protective strategy to the overall position.

And the real tragedy is that most traders who suffer this misguidance regarding the merits of ES trading eliminate the other contracts from their monitor screens altogether, and in so doing deny themselves some of the best decision support the market offers about itself every day.

At the time of this writing, and for the better of some 10 years or more that this author has been focusing on and experiencing the issue of leadership each day, the mini Russell contract (TF), leads the market. Having said that, it doesn't lead it every day, and at some market-turning junctures and trend-development drives, it blatantly lags the reversal action of the other contracts. At such times, it's as if the TF were playing a General Custer role, unable to change its trend opinion, hanging tough and giving up little or no ground until it suddenly catches up with a violence more associated with the release of an economic report. Such moments, however, tend to be more rare than not. And because the TF displays the true leadership aspect so consistently, it warrants the respect of being the default leader of choice.

Each day, however, does convey its own trend messages, and the only way to really hear this message clearly is to view each day's opening without trend prejudice, regardless of any pre-opening or overnight news that may have been released, and regardless also as to how far away from yesterday's Close did today's Open actually gap. Just open your ears and shut down your trend prejudice and listen to what the market is saying. And here's what such a listening device looks like. I use some six 19-inch LED monitors for my trading desktop, but could probably get by with just four. But even if you only have two monitors, consider setting up one of them to look like the chart screen in Figure 5.1.

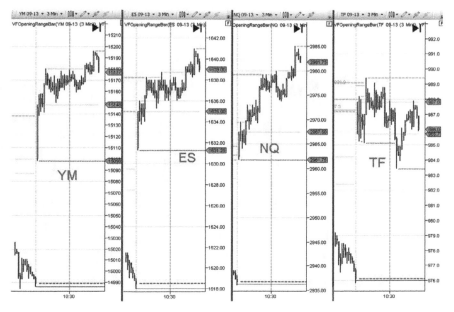

FIGURE 5.1 TF Divergence

Study the charts in Figure 5.1, from July 17, 2013. Note how the TF contract failed to confirm each new high by the other three contracts, and instead created a series of lower highs each time. We call this concept Serial Divergence™. Simple divergence would contain only one such nonconfirmation signal. The mini Russell contract seemed to know what was coming all along, as price eventually came crashing down later into the 2:30 Transition Time. (See the outcome in Figure 5.2.)

The same issue of leadership works the other way. In the chart below, note the series of lower lows made by the ES into the Noon Hour while the TF made a series of higher lows. (See Figure 5.3.)

It was the relative strength of the TF that signaled the true trend. However, the ES could have been purchased while making a new low just as easily as the TF making a higher low. (See the outcome in Figure 5.4.)

On the particular day in Figure 5.4, I happened to be visiting another vendor's chat room, which monitored and traded only the ES. Toward the end of the day, around 14:30 P.M. (2:30 P.M. ET) before the final leg up of the ES recovery rally, this trader was continually trying to short the ES. He got stopped out several times, and never succeeded in getting in sync with the true trend. One look at a TF chart could have told him which way the final minutes of the Last Hour Time Frame were to turn out.

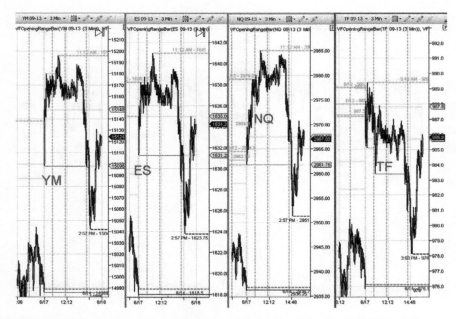

FIGURE 5.2 TF Divergence Pay-Off (as continued from Figure 5.1)

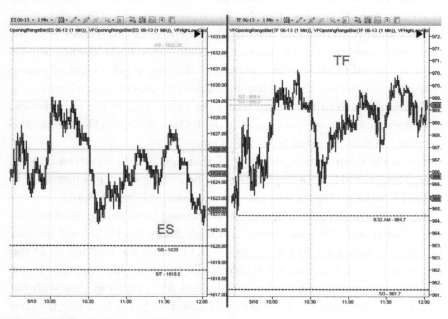

FIGURE 5.3 TF Serial Divergence

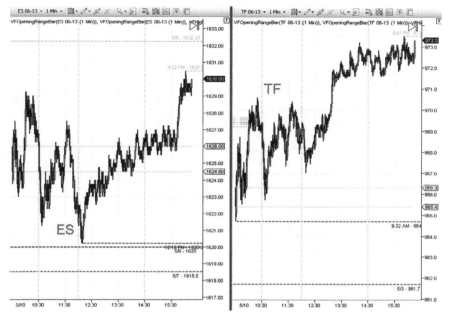

FIGURE 5.4 TF Divergence Payoff (as continued from Figure 5.3)

Sometimes the leadership is so glaring from the beginning of the 1st Frame that it almost looks like the data from the diverging contracts are streaming from entirely different days of history. On the day sampled in Figure 5.5, the ES and NQ contracts have actually returned in a small bounce back to the Opening Range while the TF contract, in total collapse, wasn't even able to gather together a recovering reversal. Something had to give. (See Figure 5.5.)

Betting against the leadership of the TF would have been unwise. In fact, this kind of leadership invites taking a position in sync with the TF's direction, but in one of the laggards, ES or NQ, as either one was far more likely to play catch-up to the TF than the other way around. See that day's outcome as continued in Figure 5.6.

A little less obvious and at times quite deceiving is the concept of Leadership Shift. In the early action of the day shown in Figure 5.7, the TF seemed to have the best chance of an early closing of its opening gap, with a series of lower lows initially ignored by the other contracts.

Shifting from a divergent role to a leadership role by TF can be one of the most powerful trend signals in the early going. It can't be predicted, and since

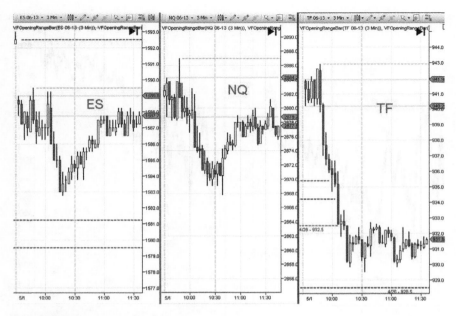

FIGURE 5.5 TF Leadership

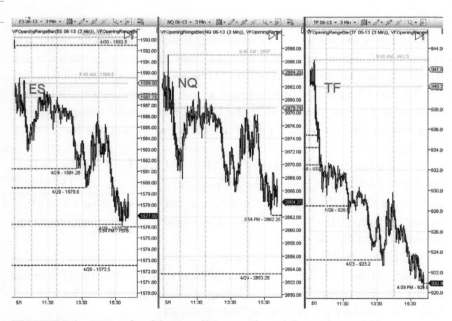

FIGURE 5.6 TF Leadership Payoff (as continued from Figure 5.5)

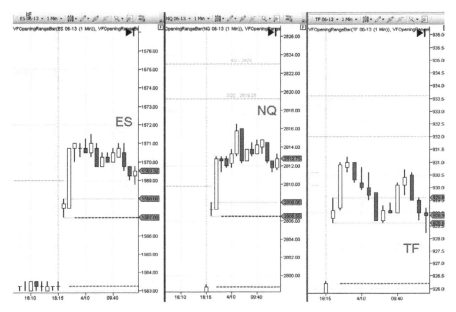

FIGURE 5.7 TF: Lagging or Leading?

it's unusual, this initial reluctance by the leader to be in sync with the others is part of a trend disguise. When the TF contract suddenly snaps into a leadership role in the direction it seemed just minutes before to resist, the trader should turn to breakout strategies quickly in the direction of the converging trend, as those who didn't believe in the trend initially because of poor leadership are now forced to play catch-up with the dramatic TF leadership emergence. Just such a shift can be studied in Figure 5.8, which is a continuance of the day that began in Figure 5.7.

Initially leading down, the TF's sudden shift to get in sync with the others should sound like an alarm bell going off in a trader's head. This simple concept is one of the most powerful signals a trader can view, and would be totally lost on someone not comparing these contracts simultaneously in the earliest minutes after the Open, and not well versed in what it means that the TF, first diverging in one direction, rapidly shifts back to leadership in the other. Leadership Shift is often an important signal for an ensuing Persistent Trend Day, introduced in a subsequent chapter.

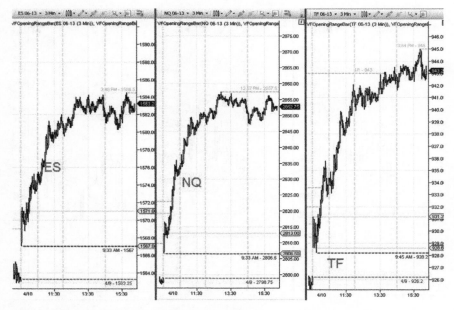

FIGURE 5.8 TF Leadership Shift (the outcome of Figure 5.7)

■ Summary

Leadership can be an invaluable tool. But the concept is worthless if you can't identify the leader. What you put on your main screen while monitoring the day becomes habitual. Learn to watch at least three of the main four stock index contracts side-by-side, with either the ES or the YM "big cap" indices as nearly replaceable, one with the other. Study the main trend reversal pivots each day. What were the separate contracts doing when these reversals got started?

CHAPTER 6

The Work-Done Concept

The intraday trader's view of market action is admittedly narrow. In fact, investors and advisors to investors who buy and hold stocks and mutual funds would consider the trends of the intraday action as no more than noise. But anyone spending serious time examining the action in the lower frames of the stock futures indices finds as much order there as a scientist might find examining nature through a microscope. Even if the exact underlying principles remain a mystery, a repetition to market behavior is unmistakable. It's on such repetition—and the leverage afforded them through exchange-regulated futures derivatives—that intraday traders capitalize.

Only in rare moments does the market take a direct route to any destination. It gives, and then it takes back. And after it takes back, it gives even more. And yet all along the way, if one examines the main index contracts closely, the market leaves signals not only that it's finished with one direction, but signposts in its wake so that when this next push onward also finds an end to its trend, price action will know how and where to find its way back to some part of the journey left behind. In an earlier chapter, we described one of these telltale signs, the Break-away Pivot, as a piece of *unfinished business* that price may want to revisit sometime before getting on with its larger underlying destiny.

The Trader must acknowledge that the market often sees itself as called back to such things as open gaps, Break-away Pivots, and previous lows and highs. He may never understand why market action can leave a sense of unfinished business to its internal structure that demands another visit, but that's not the Trader's business to understand. The Trader only wants to capitalize on the behavior and so notes the appearance of the signposts. The Trader embraces the outcome. So that a completed trend or target achievement can prompt the trader into acting on a plan, we give this phenomenon of finished business to a Trend a name. We call this concept *Work-Done*.

Every trader wants to catch trends. For our purposes, a trend is any major swing in the intraday charts of the stock index futures contracts. The best trends of the day will usually end in making a new intraday high or low, or will break out from a consolidation pattern that leads to a series of new highs or lows, behind which the trader can trail a stop-loss order as an exit strategy. These swings make up the main profit opportunities of the day.

Work-Done is usually an incomplete set of clues to a reversal signal. The concept is best used as a signal for exiting a position, needing a less stringent set of requirements to exit a trade than to enter a fresh one. Any clue or set of clues that signal a possible end-of-trend, even if incomplete, warrants at least a partial exit with profits in hand, the nature of intraday trends being so fickle. Getting back in again, especially with a position in the opposite direction, should require the appearance of additional technical concepts.

Traversing the previous day's trading range from the Y-High to the Y-Low, for instance, is easily enough of an excuse to *exit* for profits, and would therefore come under the heading of Work-Done. But *entering* a trade reversal to such an occurrence is a more weighty decision. Just because the Y-High or Low had been taken out by such a 1st Frame trend is not, in and of itself, sufficient information to fade the event, turn-and-reverse, and go the other direction. More complete information is surely necessary to enter a fresh trade. When the particular factors of time, pattern, price and/or divergence arrive simultaneously, the impetus for taking a fresh position is at hand. This more complete confluence of market phenomena is called a *Technical Trade Entry Model*, and is covered in detail in the last section of this book. The Trader categorizes the potential ingredients for such models so as to trigger an action from his Trade Plan. Having a Trade Plan of trade entry models substitutes the need for "tape reading," as it is sometimes called, and is designed to eliminate the introduction of intuition into the Trader's day.

As explained above, a precise definition of the Work-Done tool is not really possible. For the tool to be effective and useful, the rule base must be flexible. There are, nevertheless, a few specific attributes that serve to unify the variable set of conditions that go into the making of Work-Done.

A Work-Done signal can be as simple as exiting a position after an extended move into the 10:30 A.M. Trend Check or the 11:15 A.M.

FIGURE 6.1 Work-Done at the First Transition Time

Transition Time, as price often loses momentum and pattern becomes more complex. (See Figure 6.1.)

The example used in Figure 6.1 illustrates the simplest of event concepts. A number of simple technical achievements can result in the concept of Work-Done. But it's the trip getting there that's so important, not the specific achievement itself. Arriving at any of these relative price levels becomes meaningless without the exhausting trip.

Elements that make up this event concept come from price achievement, pattern fruition, and time of day, and can include:

- Achieving Daily Pivot levels, Value Area Point-of-Control

- The taking out of yesterday's High or Low (the Y-High or Y-Low), the overnight High or Low, or an intraday high or low

- Closing a Gap, or closing a Lap

- A return to the Opening Range Bar (ORB)

- A thrust through the ORB (the Kilroy)

- A return to a triangle's apex

- A return to a channel's centerline

- A completed pattern target, such as a Head-and-Shoulders, Triangle, Channel Breakout, and so forth, sometimes referred to as a Measured Move (discussed in subsequent sections)

- An achieved Inverse 78% Projection target (as discussed in Chapter 3)

- The Transition Times that end the 1st Frame and Midday Frame

- The Noon Hour High/Low, the 10:00 A.M. News Bar, the 10:30 A.M. Trend Check

- A solo new High or Low that remains unconfirmed by the other contracts

- A spike through the 200EMA or 1300EMA in the 1-minute bar frame

- Divergence between the Dow Jones index contract, the E-mini S&P, the Nasdaq and or the E-mini Russell 2000, and so forth

Keep in mind that it's the trip getting to any of these potential support/ resistance points that potentially exhausts the trend. There is no magic in any particular price number, no matter how it is derived. If the unfolding internal structure of a particular trend is not finished, then price will eventually clip one support/resistance number after another fulfilling its destiny.

For opening a fresh trade position, the Work-Done concept may only be a contributing factor. To initiate a new position, a confluence of technical concepts must be present. Although typically four or five can be present at significant intraday trend turns, at least three should be readily identifiable at the right edge of the video screen to be classed as a *Technical Trade Entry Model*. Without having these more stringent criteria, there is no distinguishing a Trade Plan from simple tape reading or market intuition. The Technical Trade Entry Model is covered in Part Four, but differs from a simple Work-Done concept in a number of ways:

- The aspects of an Entry Model come from disparate market phenomenon (not otherwise related).

- They should be dispersed between two or more of the stock market index contracts.

- They can be associated with our Time Markers, especially the transitions between one time frame and the next.

- The aspects must occur or accumulate approximately at the same time.

■ Summary

Using the Work-Done concept to identify targets for at least a part of a multi-contract trade position can help acquire far better profits in the shorter intra-day world than trailing stops. This can require an adjustment to the thinking of many traders who are used to exiting always on stop-loss orders. Think instead as exiting into the thrust of the favorable trend as any of these typical price achievement concepts listed above are being met.

Trading between *swings* as a concept is facilitated by identifying punctuation marks between one intraday trend and another. Specific technical events finish the business of trend excursion and so signal the aptly named trigger Work-Done.

CHAPTER 7

Trading the News

I've explained this technique in a number of webinars, and one of them is currently on the ValhallaFutures website. In fact, I use this method any day there is pending economic news at any of the scheduled times in the 1st Frame session, normally at 10:00 A.M. ET. In theory it could work for the Federal Reserve's rate change announcement, normally scheduled for 2:15 P.M. ET, but prices have usually been drifting for several hours in the Midday Frame rather than seeking reversals at pivots such as commonly seen in the first hour, so the afternoon scheduled economic news releases lend themselves less consistently to pre-positioning.

Most room monitors who trade futures in a chat room flatten out their positions near the time of a news release if the specific economic report is one that is anticipated for its subsequent volatility, such as the Philly Fed Manufacturing Index. This is partly on caution that they don't lead member-subscribers into positions through extremely volatile price spikes with ugly stop-loss executions, and partly because they have no real methodology to trade the news.

Since news itself is impossible to predict, and usually even less possible to truly interpret after it's released, some method vendors actually prescribe that traders bracket a nearby 5-minute bar range just before the news, with the anticipation that this method of getting a fill will capture the ensuing trend early. I'm not kidding; I actually sat through such a presentation. I guess in theory it sounds very logical, even an obvious way to participate with the outcome of the news. The problem, however, is one of fill quality. A safe use of a stop-limit order will prevent the desired fill on any volatile news announcement, and a straight stop-entry order will get filled as a market order, but almost always at the very tip of the news spike, at the worst possible place, just before it collapses back in the direction of the pre-news price. It's a guaranteed loss. Any vendor teaching such a trade setup has no real experience taking such a position with real money, as the fills would usually be so devastating.

Other vendor's teach a method that trades that same anticipated price spike but just after the news, this time trying to fill intentionally near the end of the spike, but in the opposite trend direction, back in toward the price just before the news came out. A +1,000 tick reading, a penetration outside of a Bollinger Band, moving averages, pitchfork prong, or even a regression channel extreme, could all be the entry trigger for fading the news spike. This technique has a far better chance of success than bracketing the news range with stop-entry orders in the direction of the initial breakout, but picking the sweet spot for the entry of such a post-news reversal is a task requiring a great deal of precision.[1]

That leaves only one real alternative to entering trades involving the news event: Be already positioned *before* the news comes out, and take advantage of the news spike for a profitable exit, in trend, rather than a countertrend entry after the news. The management of this position is critical to reducing risk, and is part of a specific rule set. *First*, the trade entry requires a clear reversal signal that would have fulfilled any trade plan requirements normally in place whether a news announcement was pending or not. *Second*, part of the position must have reached an initial profit object and therefore taken out to help pay for the trade, covering most of the risk of any remaining positions at their adjusted stop-loss levels. *Third*, a profit must be showing for the last positions as the last 15 to 20 seconds appear on the clock prior to the scheduled announcement. If no such premium exits on the position at that time, exit the position at the market. If one does exist, hold the position into the news with a generous limit target, possibly just a few ticks beyond the current high or low of the day's range, or the previous day's range. If the last part of the position contains multiple contracts, a much higher target could be set for that last contract with a trailing stop as the exit strategy. And *fourth*, after the news is out, and if the reaction has favored the direction of the position, move the stops on the remainder of the position to break-even at a minimum should none of the targets be reached by the budding trend.

It's amazing how many times the 10 A.M. news outcome seems anticipated by a reversal signal that occurs some 5 to 15 minutes prior to the news itself. Every time I trade this model in webinars, I get the same question. It's an obvious question, but also very revealing. "How did you know the news spike would go that direction?" Of course, there is no way to predict the news. I have no idea what it will be, nor do I even attempt to understand it.

What, you think all those floor traders in the S&P pit are so well schooled in economics that they can interpret the context, subtext, and nuance of an economic indicator, weigh it against the expected change, and in less than a few milliseconds make a decision about their entries? Impossible. And for those who think it's all rigged and the updated reports are available to insiders well before the scheduled release, I say it doesn't make any difference. If such insiders exist—and they might—they are in such small numbers, and protect themselves with such secrecy against serious felony prosecution so well, that they could never have the effect on the markets to turn all stocks, all indices, and all ETFs together at a reversal point where the market often turns before the release time anyway.

No one can move that much money. It would require a universal huddle. And in truth, the participants are in such competition with each other that no such huddle would be possible even if there were an electronic gathering place where they could line up in unison and yet somehow keep that secret intention from just you. Oh, wait. There is such a place. It's called the marketplace, and it would be wise to keep in mind that for every buyer along the way there was a seller to meet that price, and vice versa. Except perhaps for a very few cheaters, the market is a very fair—if unforgiving place.

The following example fulfilled all the critical rules of the pre-news day setup model on June 21, 2013. Study Figure 7.1. A trend had been established when price broke below the ORB sharply after first closing the previous day's gap above the ORB. This sharp breakdown left a Pivot Ledge right at the ORB, which meant there would be a double layer of resistance should the market be called back there to revisit that breakdown Ledge. I remember calling this in real-time for the chat room as a demonstration to some new members as a potential example of a pre-news model.

We took short positions as price returned to the ORB and the Pivot Ledge, and then took an initial, partial position profit of 1 point as price fell slightly into 9:59 A.M., just before the Philly Fed Manufacturing Index report was due. That 1-point profit also left some distance between the entry price and the pre-news price just 15 seconds before the news was due, providing some profit cushion for the remaining position as a whole should price spike back up sharply on the news. I had no conclusions as to the content of that report, and frankly would not be able to speak to the nuances of its interpretation anyway. Had price moved back up to my entry price in those closing moments *before* the news, eliminating that important cushion, I would have simply exited the trade and gone flat. Instead, the pre-news cushion allowed me to hold the position *into* the scheduled news release. In

FIGURE 7.1 TF Pre-News Trade Entry Setup

FIGURE 7.2 TF Pre-News Entry Payoff (as continued from Figure 7.1)

this case, it sent price sharply lower, in the direction all the technical elements would have called for the trend anyway. (See Figure 7.2.)

I took final profits on that price spike as it was breaking the Y-Low on a large potential Die Bar, just around 10:01 A.M., still several points above an eventual bull reversal took hold, some five minutes later. My net was nearly five points for both contracts, an amount about equal to my Trade Plan's profit goal for the entire 1st Frame. Exiting on the initial price spike fits the trade rules for this trade model, even if it leaves money on the table, because such price breaks often leave the unfinished business of a Pivot Ledge and a Break-away Lap in their wake. These can, and usually do call the market back up to retest the Ledge created with the news itself, and would threaten the important profits of the remaining pre-news position in the process. Intraday traders must stay disciplined and trade a plan, look for the next model to appear at the right edge of the video screen, and not worry about what trend swings go unidentified or extend far beyond one's target expectations.

Study Figure 7.2 closely again. Although it took almost an hour to get back there, price eventually did retest that Break-away Pivot created by the 10:00 A.M. news itself, before conducting further downtrend business.

In summary, this pre-news setup is really just the act of taking a position based on the technical concepts of the trade when they occur as if there was no news announcement pending at all, and exiting it quickly just *before* the news if no cushion of profits has been created by the position, or exiting *into* the news if the news plays out further to benefit the position. On many occasions with no premium cushion showing, I have exited the trade as per the rule, only to see the position move into profits from the trend signal anyway, undisturbed by the news shakeout, if any. The news only takes a minute or less to have its immediate effect. Once that effect is over, the market will proceed on toward the same trend destiny it had before the news came out. If the signal still stands as valid, and I have exited on caution that the paper profit premium was too small a cushion to risk the potential volatility, I can—and often have—stepped right back into the trade in order to position for the same potential results.

None of this strategy is possible for the Trader unless he understands and fully accepts this basic premise: **neither the news nor fundamentals lead the market.** The market leads the news, and needs no further justification for its outcome, even though the entire industry of financial news reporting and its livelihood depends on the public believing otherwise.

Understanding this premise also makes possible the complement of the pre-news trade setup; namely, the post-news trade setup. If the news volatility did nothing but hasten price onto a trend climax where target and wave fruition would be accomplished by a final push anyway, then a trade entry opportunity in the opposite direction has appeared as a reversal model in consequence. In truth, that model would have been just as valid without the news as with it, but average traders don't know that. They believe the news is the cause of a change in trend that would not have occurred otherwise.

Take the example in Figure 7.3, for instance. The reaction to good news at exactly 10:00 A.M. sent prices in all contracts up for a minute or two,

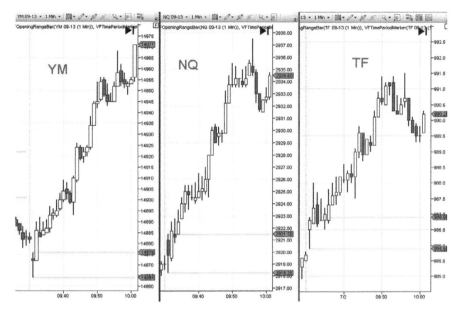

FIGURE 7.3 Post-News Trade Model

and in the process pushed the Dow Jones futures (symbol YM), but only the Dow futures, to a new high of the day (HOD).

Note that the supposed good news could only manage to drive the YM to a new high of the day, making this a Solo New HOD. The YM almost never leads. And although the trade could have been taken in either the YM or the NQ, note in the next chart, Figure 7.4, that this signal was best *borrowed* and taken in the TF, which was showing the greatest relative weakness.

Study the chart in Figure 7.3 again and ask yourself if you could have pulled the trigger at the end of that last 1-minute bar showing the YM at a fresh high. Trading around the news requires some expertise. And understanding the merits of divergence and leadership requires considerable experience watching all the main stock index contracts simultaneously on the same screen. Now consider that the payoff in Figure 7.4 is a typical post-news reaction.

Also note the need to always anticipate the exit target, as news reactions can be brief in both directions. In the chart of Figure 7.4, the TF finding support as it sold down into the ORB was the likeliest of immediate exit targets. Five minutes later, price had returned to the Pivot Ledge left by the news breakdown, and with it, all the considerable paper profits of the trade.

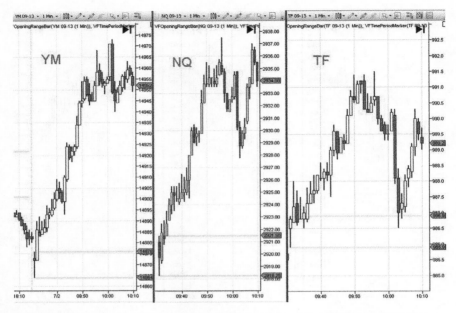

FIGURE 7.4 Post-News Trade Payoff (the continuation of Figure 7.3)

■ Summary

As my mentor Randolph Newman had to remind me many times: "The news is meant to confuse, follow the news and you will lose." That's why the best trades surrounding the news are positioned in front of it, but only if the technical aspects would support such a position anyway. Forget that the news is assumed by the majority to effect a variable outcome contingent on its own particulars. It does not change the underlying trend of the day, no matter how the financial news media may try to spin it. The outcome of the trend will eventually be the same regardless. The object is to take positions in accordance with the technical aspects of market structure if entry signals appear before the 10 A.M. news, and—depending on whether some cushion of real and paper profits has accrued from that position just prior to the new release itself—either hold the remaining position into the release, or exit it with about 20 seconds or so remaining on the clock.

On an administrative note, keep a clock-face software application with a second hand in plain view when trading the 10 A.M. news release. Make sure you have synchronized your PC clock with an Internet-time server. And forget about trading the news if your computer is on a wireless network or your Internet connection is DSL. Trading the news has additional risk considerations that require up-to-the-moment streaming data.

■ Note

1. ValhallaFutures uses a methodology called Serial Sequent Wave Method™ to identify such post-news reversals, but as a software-imbedded algorithm, is a *New School* technique, and outside the scope of this book. For a description of this methodology, see Appendix C.

PART TWO

DAY MODEL PATTERNS

If it goes up fast, it seldom lasts.

—Randolph Newman

Unless you expect the unexpected you will never find truth; so hard is it to find and grasp.

—Heraclitus

CHAPTER 8

Persistent Trend Day

In order to simplify an interpretation of the chaos otherwise known as the trading day, its seemingly unending variations in behavior patterns can be described under three broad categories: *Persistent Trend Day*, *Test-and-Reject Day*, and the *Split-Open Day*.[1] Within each of these categories, separate trade strategies are best employed for each model. Trade entry models that work in one of these *Day Model Patterns* must be avoided in another, and without an acknowledgment that one or the other of these patterns has taken hold, the chance of getting in sync with the best trade opportunities of the day is reduced. Although many trade entry models actually appear in the 1st Frame before the potential day model is understood—especially those associated with the Opening Range Bar (ORB)—the faster the day can be identified according to one of these pattern categories, the better the chance to capitalize on the opportunities the whole day offers. In other words, many valid trade entries taken around the ORB may, in fact, end up being identified later as having been countertrend, but the better trade opportunities will always be those taken in sync with the eventual trend outcome of the day.

For the chief characterizing feature of any Day-Model Pattern, we turn back to the fundamental key of the ORB. In general, price can be said to be either repelled by the presence of the Opening Range or attracted back to it. Eventually, the trend action of the day will commit to falling into just one—but apparently not both—of these attraction/repulsion properties on any one day. It's as if the ORB, acting with the properties of a magnet's duel polarity, commits to either pushing away or pulling price back, but eventually commits to one of them for the day's trend outcome.

The *Test-and-Reject Day* is the most common, and appears more than twice as often as either of the other two. It starts off in one direction, attracts a following of opinion, builds with it a kind of trend prejudice in the process, but then reverses and heads in the opposite direction, usually for the rest of the day. This model is usually associated with the most volatility of the three, and for the intraday trader, offers the best trend swing opportunities.

The least frequent of this three-pattern set is the *Split-Open Day*. In this model, price never wanders too far off its opening price, and often ends right back up where it started, leaving sometimes the infamous Doji candlestick pattern, or simply a narrow range day in the daily bars.

Occurring a bit more frequently than the Split-Open but far less frequently in any given month than the Test-and-Reject Day, is the *Persistent Trend Day*. Just as its name implies, once committed to a direction away from the ORB, it stays in this initial trend direction for the rest of the day, often relentlessly, and sometimes with few or no obvious pullbacks with which to get on board. It can have several forms. Sometimes it stalls after the Open and builds up a coil or consolidation pattern that chews up a good deal of the 1st Frame clock. Sometimes it takes off immediately from the ORB on some small and subtle breakout pattern, like those examples explored in Chapter 2. But regardless how it begins, the Persistent Trend usually ends the day making new price extremes to its initially established direction.

■ Persistence in Trend: It's a Thing

The Persistent Trend Day can be the most difficult day model of all to trade. At first glance, odd that anyone would think so. These are the days the Dow Jones Average is up 200 or more points. These are days that your neighbor, who's aware you trade for a living and secretly fancies he'd be good at it himself, calls over the fence to you when he arrives home from his office job after hearing the day's news to say something like, "Guess you had a great day, huh. Heard the market was up big all day!" "Yeah, sure," you say to yourself. "If it were only that easy. If only I could have found a place to get in. If only I had not spent the day *fading* perceived price extremes, hoping to capitalize on pullbacks that never really happened. If only I had recognized that the one sharp, stop-running, late-afternoon pullback that did finally occur would go right back into trend and onto new price extremes at the Close."

If the experience of just such a day is not in your catalogue of frustrating memories, you haven't spent any time trading the stock index futures. And to compound your frustration, it is seldom seen in the same direction two days in a row. And yet there is hope. These days do not occur without their *tells*, as they say around the poker table. And with the right mindset and a set of trade tactics, this day might yet produce your daily profit goal when it appears.

The Persistent Trend Day has character. It might not be the actor you prefer to work with, but once into its role, the persistence trait is fairly dependable. First, it commits to just one side of the ORB, an observation not particularly meaningful in the opening minutes otherwise. If the Open starts off with a gap against the previous day's Close, it's *gap-n-go*, without gap closure. If off and running quickly like that, its countertrend pullbacks tend to be shallow. The action tends to just grind onward, seemingly indifferent to the supposed magic of any number array of support/resistance levels you have established. It makes a joke of your oscillators. Those oscillator readings stay into overbought/oversold territory without producing the correction you believe they normally deserve. If there's some kind of correction near the 10:30 A.M. Trend Check, prices push on further into the trend thereafter. Fresh price extremes for the trend after a 10:30 A.M. correction act as an early signal to the potential of a Persistent Trend Day, ditto a correction near the Noon Hour High/Low. When price pushes on shortly thereafter to this Noon Hour Time Marker too, a second even stronger signal of persistence is now in place.

And those are just the objectively observable issues in the early going. The internal challenges can be even more formidable, as the following nine mental scenarios describe: (1) the early action seems to have caught you by surprise; (2) the market wasn't supposed to be doing this today; (3) admitting you're wrong here might force you to admit you've been wrong all along about the larger time frame trend; (4) yesterday seemed to confirm larger frame trend signals in the opposite direction; (5) there just has to be a better pullback than what's being offered to enter on so far; (6) it seems too late to chase it now that the quickness of the trend is already underway; (7) it can't go much further without a correction; (8) you certainly don't want to be caught chasing as that would be unprofessional; finally (9) and this the question that serves as the last refuge of all true market ignorance—was there some news or something before the market opened that I missed?

Now consider this: All the issues enumerated above, both objective and psychologically internal, and all the perplexity and conflict you face with this action *is* the tell. Accept the outcome. Your feelings and internal struggles regarding this day simply represent the crowd. You have lots of company. The countertrend trade entries of the disbelieving crowd just feed the persistent grind of the true trend direction as those positions are repeatedly stopped out. The lack of follow-through from the previous day's opposite trend direction just brings some traders to protect their profits, while others try to protect their position by adding even more to their already suffering P&L statements. There seems to be a residual, underlying momentum to this day that's secretly aligned with a larger underlying trend. Or maybe, it's the inevitability of George Douglass Taylor's three-day cycle observation[2] playing itself out as the larger time frame unfolds throughout the week.

Whatever the reason, it doesn't matter. The balance of scales is so narrowly tilted toward this one persistent direction that it looks like voting results from a national election trickling in from the polls. You have only two choices. Hold onto your capital and wait for another, more volatile, swing-oriented day, with lots of short-term overbought and oversold opportunities at either end, or wait patiently for an opportunity to participate and get in sync. Figure 8.1 exemplifies what you face.

FIGURE 8.1 Surprise, a Persistent Trend Day Up

It is of some interest to note—even in the example above—that despite the market's character of persistent grind, the 10:30 A.M. Trend Check, the Noon Hour High, and the 11:15 A.M. and 2:30 P.M. Transition Times made their presence known, but just barely. (The Noon Hour High/Low is a concept covered in Chapter 16 of Part Four, All times Eastern Standard.)

■ ORB Entries

The first and earliest way to participate in this one-way only day is to consider those ORB breakout patterns discussed in Part One. For some reason, the ORB Pennant is notorious as a possible *tell* to the Persistent Trend Day. It's a characteristic gesture with a nuclear implication. But since a Test-and-Reject reversal to the initial trend is actually the more common of day models to appear within the trading month, holding a one-lot position in expectation that a successful ORB breakout entry will go the distance of that first trend throughout the rest of the day is an improbable management strategy to collect a consistent daily profit quota. You'd be swinging for the proverbial fence. The Trader is not a gambler; he runs a business. He doesn't care about being right. His job is to ring the cash register. But if the Trader has developed a cushion of profits from a going concern, the business can handle a multiple-contract position. Let the third or fourth or fifth part of the position run. Keep a very loose trailing stop, perhaps well back beyond the protection of the ORB itself, and target not a specific price, but a specific time. Consider only trailing the stop if price successfully continues to trend as one Time Marker ticks on past another. Exit this last unit of the position at the Close. See Figure 8.2.

(You can peruse other examples at the Wiley companion website for this book, with instructions in Appendix A.)

■ Telltale Leadership

Leadership is a hallmark of the Persistent Trend Day. It is rare that all four contracts leap off in unison into the great unknown. If an ORB breakout pattern appeared from the repertoire of the previous chapters, then it doesn't really matter. You'll have a chance to participate with that contract regardless of when the others tag along. But often, no recognizable ORB breakout pattern appears at all. And if, instead, you were to take as a mindless strategy the first ORB breakout action every

FIGURE 8.2 An ORB Pennant Triggers to a Persistent Trend

day, treating each day like a potential Persistent Trend, you'd start your day's profit quota in the hole some 7 days out of 10. If instead, when the leadership of a single contract seems to get away from you—continuing to push on despite a total lack of participation by the other contracts—chances are, after a time building up a coil or consolidation pattern of some kind, the other market index sectors will follow. It's the mini Russell that usually does this leading. And on such days of solo, lonely, and even incongruous leadership, it is often not until after the first Persistent Trend Day confirmation by the lonely leader TF when the others get in sync with the trend at all. That first trend confirmation signal by the leader is simply another push of price to new trend extremes after a 10:30 A.M. pause or pullback. It's easy to understand the reluctance of the Trader to chase the leader at such times. But if in a Persistent Trend Day, the others will play catch-up, and so their laggard action is actually an opportunity to participate in the day, with entry targets as pullbacks to the ORB, as in Figure 8.3.

Note further in Figure 8.3 where the market was when the 2:30 Transition Time arrived for the TF contract. The setup you see there is kind of a *Last Chance Texaco*, as described later in this chapter.

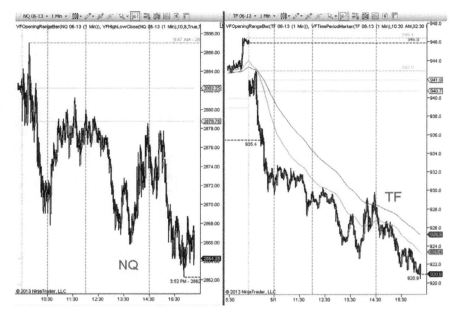

FIGURE 8.3 Pullback Entry Opportunities in the Laggards

■ Leadership Shift

Leadership is not always an obvious thing. As discussed in Chapter 5, sometimes it's disguised and a *sleeper*. Since clues to the arrival of a Persistent
Trend Day are scant and subtle, any hint that one has arrived is noteworthy.
On such days when the concept of *Leadership Shift* appears, the usual leader
will simply seem reluctant to assume the role. The mini Russell might appear
to hang back while the others have taken up the cause of the trend. It might
even appear to be trying to lead the other way. However, no distinct accom-
plishment in the opposite direction seems to be taking place as it would on
days of extreme, solo leadership divergence. It's not like the distinct and
even amazing performance depicted by the chart example in Figure 8.3, for
instance. Instead, it looks more like a little probing in the opposite direction
to the other index sectors, as in Figure 8.4.

But once in sync and matching highs for highs, the shift from one of lagging back to one of superior relative strength is a very strong signal that a
Persistent Trend Day is afoot, as in the outcome to the setup of Figure 8.4,
now seen in Figure 8.5.

FIGURE 8.4 TF Leadership Throws Head-Fake First

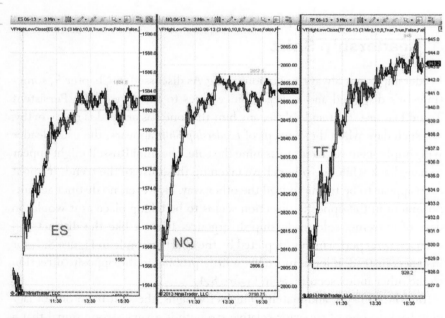

FIGURE 8.5 TF Recaptures the Leadership (a continuance from Figure 8.4)

The charts in Figure 8.4 are actually taken from the same day as our first example of the Persistent Trend Day, Figure 8.1. The subtle but effective signal of the Leadership Shift now makes the difficulty in catching the trend early on a bit less intimidating. And watching the early action with an open but practiced eye to the suddenness of this Day Model against a noted list of Trade Entry Model characteristics can help alleviate the troubling internal conflicts the Trader must face to enter positions in the direction of a runaway trend.

■ Flubber Bounce/Monkey Bars

Early in Chapter 1, we noted that there's a kind of *yin-yang* alternative to the character of the 1st Frame. Usually, it's the 1st Frame that displays an initial trend, and the Midday Frame that consolidates. But on some days, and with some forms of the Persistent Trend Day, the yang gets out in front, and the 1st Frame is occupied in coiling up until the Midday Frame takes over and uncovers the trending outcome.

On just such yang days as this, the ORB can give up its pull on contract pricing very reluctantly. In fact, it's not until price has revisited the magnet of the ORB several times that a trend can actually be uncovered. For this particular example, the return back to the ORB is usually with three distinct spikes. The volatility of the move back to the ORB has an effect of shaking confidence in the trend away from the ORB, and encourages the belief that a trend reversal is about to take place and break through the ORB to the other side altogether. This is so typical of the deceptive truth of the underlying trend. Or, has our philosopher Heraclitus so aptly observed, "Nature loves to hide."

With each return to the ORB, a loss of stored ORB magnetism is apparently taking place, or, to phrase it more vividly, with each return more energy from the ORB seems transferred to the impending trend, as if from one living thing to another. Then, when the trend finally does begin, usually after the third such return to the ORB, the trend away from it becomes decisive and persistent. After that, there is no looking back and no need to revisit. The term *Monkey Bars* is derived from the action that seems to hang price action from the overhead bars of a swing set, until—at the end of the structure—gravity wins over and pulls price off the rungs and downward into trend, as in Figure 8.6.

FIGURE 8.6 ES Monkey Bars Swing, then Persistence Down

Before turning to the next example, turn back to the chart in Figure 8.2 and consider that the TF graph in that chart comes from data gathered on the same day as the ES in Figure 8.6. Without an understanding of TF leadership, shorts taken by the ES at the ORB would have been more mentally challenging.

We take the term for the bull version of this 1st Frame coiling action, *Flubber*, from the Disney movie of same name. Here, the quick dropping-back action to the ORB is far more sudden and impulsive looking than the persistence of the climb back up. The beginner trader relying on tape reading, intuition and "feel," will often misinterpret the comparative volatility of the return back to the ORB as the truer trend determinant, and the subsequent grinding climb back up as weakness, just as the deceptive nature of this day model prescribes. Indeed, the market loves to hide its true intent. Note in Figure 8.7 how with each bounce price has ever more energy to finally leave the tugging influence of the ORB into the day's real trend destiny.

FIGURE 8.7 Flubber Bounce to Persistence Up

■ Last Chance Texaco: The 200EMA Entry

If none of the signals, patterns, or entry opportunities of the Persistent Trend Day can be recognized and acted upon in the 1st Frame there is usually one more chance to participate in the trend. Sometime deep into the Midday Frame, even into the Last Hour Time Frame of the day, a correction usually takes place to the relentless advance of the Persistent Trend. The correction is usually deep enough to have been very profitable for a countertrend trade, but the reversal at the extreme price of the Persistent Trend usually defies being identified accurately. Oscillators and various rulers of divergence and nonconfirmation work poorly or are totally dysfunctional as valid reversal signals on a Persistent Trend Day, so that countertrend fade entries usually fail repeatedly. Instead, the trader's mind becomes conditioned all day by pullbacks that dry up quickly, and then push on to new trend extremes. When a correction does finally appear, it remains unrecognizable until it's too well underway to be entered for a countertrend profit. But that doesn't mean this temporary reversal can't be used for a position in-trend at the most likely place for the correction to finish.

FIGURE 8.8 The 1-Minute Bar 200EMA Entry

Like the repeated return-to-the-ORB of the Monkey Bars and Flubber Bounce pattern action, the return to the 1-minute bar 200EMA on a Persistent Trend Day is usually characterized by a sharp price spike back inward toward the direction of ORB. The speed and acceleration of this day's solo correction usually comes at a pace designed to discourage the Trader, and convince him that a much-awaited entry opportunity to the trend has unfortunately now become a valid reversal trend instead. But the initial break of the 200EMA usually acts like a kind of trampoline to the corrective action, sending price back into the direction of the Persistent Trend as fast as it came crashing against it, as in Figure 8.8. (Colorized version of Figure 8.8 available on the Wiley companion website, with access instructions in Appendix A.)

The target of the 200EMA entry is always a new price extreme in the prevailing trend. But an important filter is considered before taking this trade. If this day model is the second Persistent Trend Day in a row in the same direction as the day before, it is far more likely that the 200EMA will not produce the expected bounce, but instead only trigger further reversal action to the prevailing persistent trend, possibly into a full correction, perhaps even back beyond the ORB. If on the other hand, this 200EMA correction appears on a second Persistent Trend Day in a row of the *opposite direction*, it tends to actually enhance the potential success of this Last Chance Texaco entry. See Chapter 11, "Day Model Sequence Cycle," for more on the subject of Day Model rotation.

Further trend signal considerations to the behavior of price as it enters *the cup* between the 200EMA and 89EMA are reviewed in Part Three, in Chapter 15, "MA Pattern Concepts."

Summary

There is typically a kind of yin-yang comparison of action of the 1st Frame to that of the Midday Frame. The 1st Frame tends to trend with volatility, while the Midday Frame tends to relax into consolidation. And accordingly, there are these two distinct Persistent Trend Day setups that correspond. One seems launched into a strong trend immediately after an ORB break-out, and the other coils back to the ORB repeatedly until energized enough to jettison away from the ORB's magnetic orbit for the rest of the day.

Luckily, not all contracts exhibit either of these two behaviors in the early going on the same day, so that the signals in the leader might eventually be applied to entries in the laggards. And as a Last Chance Texaco to the day, price will often come ripping back through the 200EMA (as applied to 1-minute bars) to gobble up stop-loss orders like the little video game *Pac-Man*. If occurring on the first Persistent Trend Day in several days, this pull-back action usually reverses right back into trend to finish making new price extremes near the Close of the day. But if the day in question is the second Persistent Model in a row of the same direction, chances are very high that a correction to this second Persistent Trend Model will not spring price back into trend, but instead carry much deeper than the 200EMA, and even likely work itself into a full reversal back to the ORB or beyond.

Notes

1. The definitions of these terms are specific to this text and are not meant to reflect similar terms by other authors. Grant Noble's *Split Open* bears no resemblance to this term, and instead it is used by Grant to describe when today's price opens within the prior day's Settlement Price Range. Larry Levin and James Dalton also make use of the concept of day modeling in their work, but again, their descriptive definitions differ. See the Bibliography.
2. George Douglass Taylor, *The Taylor Trading Technique* (Greenville, SC: Traders Press, 1950).

CHAPTER 9

Test-and-Reject Day

The Test-and-Reject Day Model is the most common of the three Day Model Patterns and appears more than twice as much as either of the other two put together. Generally speaking, price heads off away from the Opening Range Bar (ORB) seeking a trend and taking the bulk of traders and their sentiment as to trend with it. In other words, this first trend direction of the day, even though usually doomed, is nonetheless quite convincing. But just about the time everyone has gotten the message as to the extent and direction of the trend, it runs out of gas, and becomes unable or unwilling to extend beyond this first main fractal of wave patterns at some identified level of support/resistance. Then, price reverses and makes the trip back to the ORB where it began, and then usually beyond. The action, pattern, and persistence regarding price back at the ORB becomes the hallmark and confirmation that a Test-and-Reject Day is at hand. The Trader sees these turning points as swings and trade opportunities. Tools as to how to help identify that this first trend is false will be added continually in the text to follow, in this chapter and those thereafter.

ORB Breakout plays are not married to the Persistent Trend Day alone. As there are far more Test-and-Reject Days than Persistent Trend Days, the Trader must trail his final units of any breakout position with an eye to understanding the probabilities that favor an eventual reversal. And it should not be otherwise. Why would an intraday trader give up all the profits from a small position, or the paper profits of a 1-lot position as yet unrealized for the sake of an assumption that this breakout play has landed in the less probable of Day Model outcomes? To the extent this conflicts with the goal of trailing a final position from an initial ORB breakout play into the less-likely end-of-day price extreme offered by the less-frequent Persistent Trend Day Model is but a reflection on the size capabilities and risk tolerance of the individual trader. Those trading with only one to three contracts will always find it difficult to risk a final contract on an end-of-day outcome. The trader with five to 10 contracts—not so much.

This Test-and-Reject Day Model, then, can be divided into 1st and 2nd Trend Directions for selecting specific Trade Entry Models for execution. Since the 1st trend is false, no matter how convincing, identifying the clearest reversal opportunity might position a trader for capturing a good segment of the best profit opportunity of the 1st Frame and sometimes the rest of the day. And since the 2nd Trend Direction is the truer trend of the Test-and-Reject Day, the 2nd Trend Direction deserves more respect. Looking for it to end prematurely with trades back in the direction of the initial 1st Trend will usually result in quick stop-outs. If the Work-Done concept can be associated with the completed business of the 1st Trend, this 2nd Direction becomes far riskier to fade, and far safer in which to trade in sync. After all, once identified correctly, trades taken in the direction of the 1st Trend are actually counter-trend to the outcome of the day. Instead, further 2nd Trend Direction breakouts and pullbacks as in-trend entries will show the better profits and offer the lower risk setups.

The Test-and-Reject Day Model is associated with some of the more volatile price action of the three. That shouldn't be hard to understand. The reversal of this model catches so many traders by surprise. A good cross-section of market participants are stopped out of one set of trade commitments, only to be forced to reorient those commitments back in the opposite direction. Just as many participants fighting the burgeoning 2nd Trend will repeatedly add to their original 1st Trend commitments as if to protect them, but ultimately face the same consequence, adding even more heat to the developing reversal action. On a Test-and-Reject Day, once the reversal is in place, resistance is futile.

The difficulty and frustration felt by many regarding this 2nd Trend Direction of the day is often very intense and cannot be overstated. It seems that the very nature of the market is designed to conflict with our expectations and therefore our emotions. To illustrate this point, floor traders themselves, who are normally thought of as the most savvy, are very susceptible to acquiring prejudice towards this 1st Trend Direction when experiencing a particular exhausting morning of price waves, one more deeper than another. "Paper," as they call it, has continued pummeling them with order pressure from off-floor. News reports stimulate the trend, and pullbacks continually seem to give way to new price extremes. Eventually, the message just gets pounded home. The trend has been established to the first direction, or so it seems.

I once trained with a very savvy floor trader who served as an analyst to the Swiss Franc pit, and then to the S&P pit just after that pit's initial opening back in the early 1980s. Every day he'd walk around the pit to chat briefly with some established floor traders with whom he was well acquainted. But quietly, he was actually taking a poll. After speaking to nearly a dozen or so by the end of the first 45 minutes, he'd tally the results. And then, to my total amazement, he'd begin calling trades in the opposite direction to the consensus of the day's trend opinions. "Floor traders?" I asked. "You fade floor traders?"

I left that day's training stunned. And even though his actions only mirrored what my earlier mentor from the New Orleans Cotton Exchange had oft repeated to me before, that *everybody* was always wrong, I never thought to associate it with the savvy experience of floor traders.

The proverbial light bulb finally went on one day while listening to a taped lecture by the then soon-to-be author Mark Douglas, of *The Disciplined Trader* fame.[1] Pregnant with meaning in all its simplicity, I digest his thoughts into the following premise.

The Douglas Premise
Most of the money lost in the markets is lost by traders who thought they knew which way the market was *supposed* to go.

The impetus behind the mindset of many traders is a desperate want for a piece of the trend they initially missed in the 1st Trend Direction. And so, it is natural for these same traders to assume the ensuing action of the first big pullback as but an opportunity to get in sync with the trend just missed. It is this very nature of growing surprise to the retracement of the day's first trend that characterizes one of the early tells of the Test-and-Reject day. Something just isn't right about the pullback. *It just keeps growing.*

The Trader has to listen at such times, has to go back to the charts and look for signs that a top or bottom to the initial action has actually been put in place. The Trader must recognize the possibility that the needed work of the initial trend has been done—that is, the Trader must be aware of *Work-Done* technical aspects

The characteristics of Work-Done identification can greatly add to the recognition of a change to the initial trend of the day. And if identified successfully, the Trader has a much better chance of getting in sync with the budding 2nd Trend Direction before too much capital has been expended attempting to fight it. The Trader must now visualize new targets in the opposite direction, and find entries within a Trade Plan that will navigate such contingencies. The Trader must turn the screen upside down, flip his or her hat around backwards—or even turn a sock inside out.

You think I'm kidding? Trend prejudice comes from a deep-seated need in all of us to be in the right. It's partly a powerful need to display our acumen, to control our destiny, and to prove we can beat the intellectual challenge presented to us each day by the market's innate trend disguise. As a corollary to this, there is nothing more difficult in nature than to admit to being wrong. It has a mental chain reaction of reaching back to topple many other things we might then have to admit we were also wrong about, much like a stand of dominoes. But the Trader remains always humble with the positions he takes. He has learned to enter his trades based not on a belief of correctness about trend, but on the reappearance of repetitive models at the right edge of his video screen.

My old mentor Randy used an interesting turn of phrase when stressing to me the importance of the first reversal of the day and the hidden power of the 2nd Trend Direction. Typically he'd say, "Now position yourself to be surprised." The Trader must learn to quickly reposition himself to benefit from his own surprise.

Corollary #1 to the Douglas Premise

If most of the money lost in the markets is lost by traders who thought they knew which way the market was supposed to go, then most of the money to be made in the markets is made at the places where most traders are proven wrong and stopped-out.[2]

In the chart example in Figure 9.1, the TF contract is opening gap-up on a day following a Persistent Trend Day Up. Only rarely are there ever two Persistent Trend Days back-to-back in the same direction. This is a very important technical trend attribute, and earns an emphasis of its own in a subsequent chapter.

On this day, the Open is finishing some business left undone from previous price action. It's closing an open gap from two days prior, Work-Done. It was only natural that prices would then fall back and—keeping

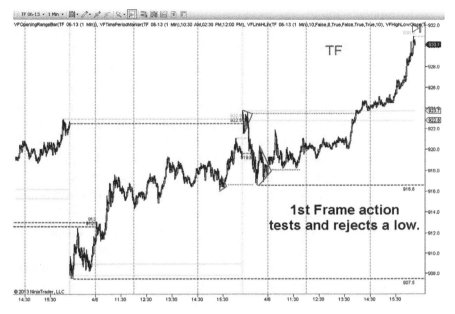

FIGURE 9.1 Work-Done Brackets the 1st Trend

within a cycle rotation of rally and correction—find itself in an immediate position to begin correcting. Note too that on a potential Test-and-Reject day, price immediately created an ORB Pennant, encouraging a sell-short trigger-entry a tick or two below the pennant to participate in the earliest move of the day's potential correction.

Lower down, after testing support from the 2:30 Transition Time of the day before, where the apex of another small breakout pennant extended into the day at hand, the TF contract reversed by means of yet another fresh pennant of its own, right from the new day's 10:30 A.M. Trend Check. Consider that retest of the previous day's pennant apex and Break-away Pivot from the previous day's 2:30 Transition Time Marker as Work-Done again, and a logical exit target for any remaining short positions taken from the bearish ORB Pennant breakdown.

And just because there are almost never two Persistent Trend Days in a row in the same direction doesn't mean the market can't finish higher two days in a row. In fact, when trending strongly in the daily frame, the market can finish higher 8, 10, and even occasionally 12 days in row, alternating in Day Model types with intraday corrective action, like that seen in Figure 9.1, cycling through repeatedly all the way.

To complicate things, the swing volatility of the Test-and-Reject Day might send prices to Work-Done zones at both ends before deciding on a final trend direction. This can actually mean price will crisscross the ORB in both directions, without committing to the 2nd Trend on the initial reversal. On such days, price might reject a small initial trend, then crash through the ORB only to accomplish some more significant Work-Done at the opposite end, starting the process of Test-and-Reject all over again. All of this initial pricing might yet be considered the 1st Trend Direction of the day, even though it included a zigzag through the ORB. The more serious and significant the business finished in one direction, the more likely the true trend to be uncovered in the other. And in the end, the direction of the previous Persistent Trend Day will usually reassert itself; if not on the first Test-and-Reject Day following the Persistent Trend, then the day after. Chapter 11, "Day Model Sequence Cycles," will explore this subject in detail.

Note the Work-Done accomplished in the chart of Figure 9.2, in which the previous day's gap, the Y-Low and then the Globex Low, were all taken out before a firm reversal took place and started back up.

As stated earlier, the Test-and-Reject Day Model is characterized by a greater volatility than the other two Day Models under discussion in this

FIGURE 9.2 The YM Uncovers the True Trend

section, the Persistent Trend Day and the Split-Open Day. And since swings are the food of the intraday opportunity, Test-and-Reject Days offer the best opportunity for intraday swing trades, assuming the Trader understands and lives by Time Markers, Work-Done concepts, and furthermore, respects the power of established 2nd Trend Directions in his or her trade entry tactics.

It should be stressed here that the Trader's role is not one of a predictor. He doesn't have to know how far a 2nd Trend Direction reversal might take the new trend. His job is to position when Work-Done aspects have been accomplished.

More examples of this Day Model are displayed in subsequent chapters, as additional trade concepts are explained in relation to a greater whole, especially in Part Three, "Repetitive Chart Patterns." A hallmark of the Test-and-Reject Day Model is the appearance of 1st Trend price rejection in the form of classic chart-pattern reversals, such as the Triangle, Head-n-Shoulders, W-Bottom, M-Top, Cup-n-Saucer, and so forth. An association of these patterns with the Test-and-Reject concept makes this Day Model much easier to trade. For instance, note the dotted red lines in the example of Figure 9.2. An M-Top Reversal helped identify price rejection of the highs, and an Inverse Head-n-Shoulders Bottom did the same for the lows.

For additional examples typical of Test-and-Reject, go to the book's companion website, with instructions in Appendix A.

▓ Summary

On more days in the stock index market than otherwise, the initial trend away from the ORB gets reversed into a truer trend of the opposite direction. This Test-and-Reject Day Model is associated with more volatility, more pattern formation, more reversals, stronger punctuation between transition times, more use and variety of technical indicators and patterns, and accordingly more opportunity for the intraday trader. As we progress through the explanation of additional technical concepts, the opportunities to trade the Test-and-Reject Model will become more apparent.

▓ Notes

1. Mark Douglas, *The Disciplined Trader* (Paramus, NJ: New York Institute of Finance, Simon & Schuster, 1990).

2. The Douglas Premise is not a direct quote from the work of Mark Douglas, but I believe it to be a fair assessment of his main premise. I'm not sure my corollaries would meet with his approval, but in any case, here is an excerpt quoted from the recorded lectures on which the premise is derived:

> Now those are the typical errors that a typical trader makes all the time. . . . Take those errors away and you'll become consistent winners. So why did you make the errors? . . . These errors are all essentially the result of—at one level or another—you believing that you know what will happen next. But . . . you don't know what will happen next. And this is what really separates the pros from everyone else. They don't indulge themselves into thinking they know what's going to happen next.
>
> —Mark Douglas, Dow Jones Seminars, Annual TAG Conference, Las Vegas, Nevada 1998 (Cassettes issued by Tim Slater, Telerate Seminars, New Orleans, Louisiana, but no longer reproduced.)

CHAPTER 10

The Split-Open Day

On most days, the Opening Range Bar (ORB) can be said to repel price initially into trend exploration. If the initial trend experiment doesn't work, price flips back across the ORB and tries the other. But on a Split-Open Day, price displays a repeated attraction to the ORB from both sides. It's a safety zone. And since neither trend direction seems to have merit, the ORB becomes the center of the day's action.

This is not necessarily bad for the intraday trader. Although volatility is usually reduced, fading the trend at support/resistance zones from either side tends to bring price back to the ORB as a profit target.

The key is to identify as early as possible a potential narrow range day. There are a number of clues to help identify this model early in the 1st Frame. In general, the model is one where price trades away from both sides of the ORB early in the session, an occurrence sometimes referred to by floor traders as two-sided trading. By our definition, price has not actually moved away from the ORB if any part of the current 1-minute price bar is still actually touching the ORB itself. And for the purposes of this book, the term *Split Opening*[1] refers to an opening behavior model wherein 1-minute price bars crisscross the ORB three times or more within the 1st Frame time period, as seen in Figure 10.1.

If price is this hesitant about an initial trend at the opening, chances are that action will remain trendless most of the day, or at least throughout the 1st Frame and Midday Frame. The best trades on such days are made at or through the established, intraday highs and lows. This is not so different than on a Test-and-Reject Day, which often targets a previous day's high or low before reversing back toward the ORB.

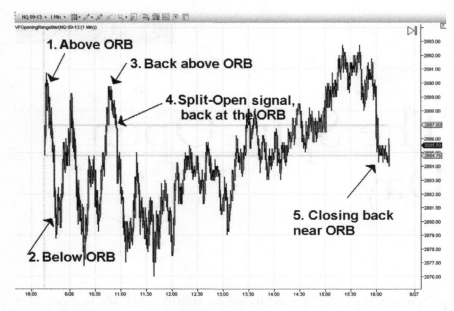

FIGURE 10.1 Price Triggers a Narrow Range Day Signal

■ Summary

The market alternates between expansion and contraction, between trend and consolidation, between volatility and relative calm. The Split-Open Day Model can be said to be the culmination of contraction within this cycle rotation. However, since the investment instrument of choice here is the highly leveraged stock index futures contract, this day need not pass without its own trade opportunities.

■ Note

1. The term *Split Opening* has long been used by traders in the grain pits to describe a specific type of opening. Grant Noble mentions it briefly in his book, *The Trader's Edge*. It occurs when today's Open falls within the narrow price range of the previous day's closing range, called the Settlement Close. The Settlement Close has no real relevance to the stock index futures contracts. This author has reused the term Split-Open but with a new definition unique to this work. See Grant Noble, *The Trader's Edge* (Chicago, IL: Probus Publishing, McGraw Hill, 1994).

CHAPTER 11

Day Model Sequence Cycle

George Douglass Taylor's much-analyzed work, which he referred to as his "Book Method,"[1] reveals the observation that the market works in short-term cycles or, stated from another viewpoint, the progress of trends unfolds in waves, each set of waves completing a fractal or segment of the trend. Having studied the Taylor method early in my career, I found I was only able to make it work if I was willing to suspend Taylor's 3-Day Cycle for a day or two completely, and then reinstate it as some fresh, new Buy-Day Low would present itself. With that modification, the 3-Day Cycle often sets up again for another rotation before falling apart once more. Linda Bradford Raschke has apparently made similar adjustments, but nonetheless once stated in a white paper that it was one of her main trading concepts.[2]

In simplest terms, the cycle consists of a Buy Day, followed the next day with a Sell Day for profit taking and, finally, on the third day, with a Sell Short Day to capitalize on the propensity for a pullback. (See Figure 11.1.)

The Sell Short Day of the one 3-Day Cycle can also become the Buy Day of the next, if the correction is deep enough and meets with some reversal criteria at the lows, as seen in Figure 11.1.

The use and understanding of Day Model Patterns is not meant to be derivative of Taylor's work, but rather to provide some recognition of how these models succeed each other from day to day, and how they can be essential to the intraday trader.

For instance, seldom does one Persistent Trend Day Model follow another in the same direction. The appearance of Persistent Trend action in the same

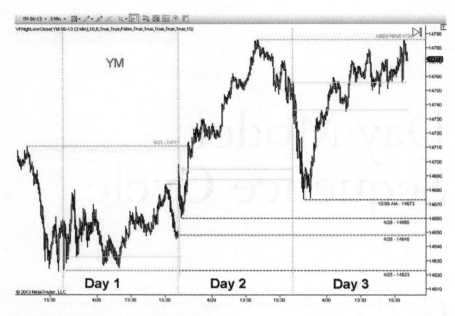

YM

Day 1   Day 2   Day 3

FIGURE 11.1 Taylor's 3-Day Cycle

direction in the 1st Frame for a second day in a row usually results in a strong reversal immediately or later in the day, as in Figure 11.2.

When a Persistent Trend Day Model does succeed itself two days in a row, it's usually—and fairly consistently—in the opposite direction. In an established bull trend, for instance, a Persistent Trend Day Down can often be followed immediately by a Persistent Trend Day Up, as in Figure 11.3.

At the very least, when a single Persistent Trend Day appears in the opposite direction to the prevailing monthly time frame trend, a reversal day of some kind, whether Persistent Trend or Test-and-Reject, will usually follow immediately to take price back in the direction of the larger trend.

The background to these trend whipsaws must be understood for what it really is to the trader, lest it become influential. Within a bull market, on the day of the persistent selling counter-trend action itself, all the financial news announcers will be interviewing fund managers, analysts, and floor traders about why that particular day supports a thesis that the market has finally signaled a larger reversal for the weeks ahead. And on the following day, in the midst of persistent buying, all those then being interviewed are of the bullish persuasion and no bears are interviewed to talk about their

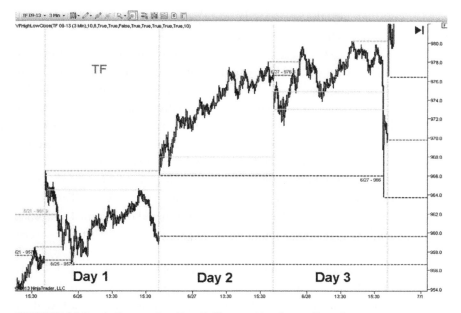

FIGURE 11.2 A Corrective Day Follows a Persistent Trend

FIGURE 11.3 Persistence Down Flips to Persistence Up

market opinions, as if the previous day didn't even exist. This is how financial journalism works: **the markets drive the news**.

An important *model sequencing signal* to note in the daily frame occurs during a bull market when a Persistent Trend Day Up is actually followed by a Persistent Trend Day Down, as it is usually the other way around in the bull phase. This change of pattern sequence usually means a change of trend in the daily frame, or the beginning of a trading range. Most traders don't recognize this as something intrinsic to internal market structure. Rather, they attribute changes like this to fundamental news that serves as the "cover story." And nothing is better cover story copy than the actions of the Federal Reserve, or its counterpart in the European Central Bank. They can't allow their Efficient Market Theory to go unsupported or be attacked. What excuse would they have for a job in financial journalism if their theory were successfully debunked?

The four index contracts followed for this book's methods—the ES, YM, NQ, and TF—do not necessarily make the same pattern model on the same day. This in itself can be a signal for the day, and even perhaps a few days further out. Compare the two pattern models in the charts in Figure 11.4. NQ has reached a full fractal in its initial move to close the gap, a potential Test-and-Reject pattern, and yet the TF contract has been unable to trade

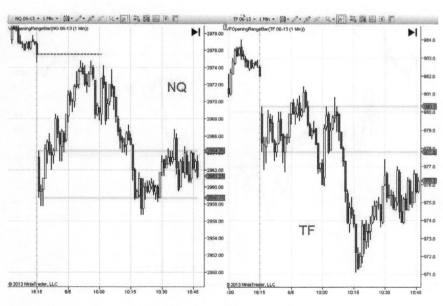

FIGURE 11.4   TF and NQ 1st Frame Setup

a single 1-minute bar above the Opening Range Bar (ORB), and instead broke down below it. (Remember, by our definition, both the low and high of a 1-minute bar must be beyond the ORB for it to qualify as having traded outside that key range.)

The eventual outcome of a Test-and-Reject is often the same as the Persistent Trend. And in this case, since the TF is the default leadership candidate, its inability to get above the ORB was a great sell signal to fade the action of the NQ as it closed its gap. It was if as the market was saying, "Okay, that business is finished, now let's follow the leader." (See Figure 11.5.)

After all, there's no certain reason that the NQ has to end its rally simply because it got to the previous day's Close. On any other day, it might keep right on going higher. It was the TF's inability to get above the ORB that revealed the true *tell* to the underlying trend.

For the record, the Test-and-Reject model in the NQ on that day was followed on the succeeding day in the NQ by a Persistent Trend Day Down, getting more in sync with the TF leadership. The TF contract did the same, making it two Persistent Trend Days in a row in the same direction for the mini Russell, but only one in a row for the NQ. That made

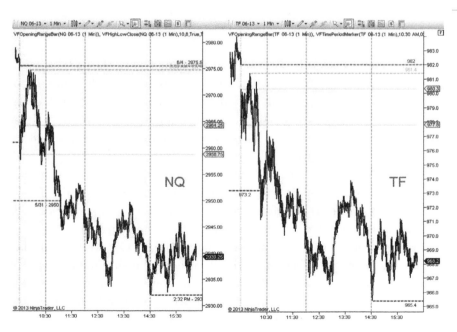

FIGURE 11.5 TF's Persistent Trend Down Leads the Way

a reversal sometime the next day even more likely. But two Persistent Trend Days seldom follow each other in the same direction, back to back. When they do, a reversal of some kind is even more likely to follow on the day after.

Figure 11.1, earlier in this chapter, contained a typical example of Taylor's 3-Day Cycle. Try to think of it, however, in terms of what might precede and follow a Persistent Trend Day. Day 1, Taylor's Buy Day of the 3-Day Cycle, serves to contain the selling of the previous day, either by reversal or simply consolidation. The Buy Day entry could come at the end of a Persistent Trend Day Down, anticipating the cycle to reverse back upwards on the following day, or even start with an opening gap up. Or, the Buy Day could simply be a Split-Opening model, wherein prices consolidate and contain the previous day's selling.

Day 2 is Taylor's Sell Day, and our Persistent Trend Day Up model. For the overnight swing trader, who established his position on Day 1, his goal is to trail growing profits with a loose stop, with an eye to being out of the position at the end of the day, or at the Open on the following day, should he want to risk a favorable Open with a position held overnight again. For the intraday swing trader who starts out flat each day, a Persistent Trend Day is the day to take breakout trades in the direction of the trend, hold a runner from an early ORB breakout trade, or buy on pullbacks when given the opportunity, but avoid counter trend fades, as the trend, so named, tends to stay persistent.

A lot of money is lost by intraday traders trying to fade the endless grind of bull markets on Persistent Trend Days because their tools continue to point to supposedly overbought conditions all along the way. On such days, countertrend traders may actually be contributing to the persistence of the trend. Their stop-loss orders, which cover their shorts at a loss, just add to the buying at higher highs.

And finally, Day 3 is Taylor's Short Day. This is typically the day after a Persistent Trend Day Up. If price starts off trying to continue in the direction of the Persistent Trend of the day before, chart reversal patterns could provide Short Sale entry triggers, typical of a Test-and-Reject Day.

It is important, however, to appraise the third day's Open relative to the Close of the Persistent Trend Day Up. If instead of further initial strength into a potential chart pattern reversal, a big gap-down opening might appear. Sometimes a good deal of the anticipated price correction to the previous day's Persistent Trend Up takes place in the overnight session action that created that gap, as in Figure 11.6.

FIGURE 11.6 A Gap Down Provides the Correction

In other words, the expected reversal against the Persistent Trend direction took place, alright, but the big gap-down opening already did most of the work, leaving the rest of the day to get back into trend with the direction of the previous Persistent Day. The correction is already over at the Open. This gap-down opening can, in fact, create the possibility of making another Persistent Trend Day back up in the same direction. If so, the intraday trader must be willing to revert to the trade entry tactics employed on the previous day. **Accept the outcome.** Taylor's cycle of rally and correction is still present, but the results might be fulfilled within the price patterns of the overnight time frame. And there is really no limit to how many days in a row a market can actually finish up or down. The presence of a cycle only serves to explain the repetitive process of wave swings, not the eventual excursion distance in the larger daily frame.

■ Summary

Since the 3–5 day cycle is inconsistent as to its start and stop point, it is easier to key trade strategies off the occurrence of a Persistent Trend Day. When the general trend of the larger weekly time frame is up, then most of the time, a Persistent Trend Day Down will be followed immediately by a reversal, often in the form of a Persistent Trend Day Up. With such awareness, the intraday trader can have a huge leg up on his strategy plans. Limiting the possibilities of what that reversal day might look like can simplify the recognition of Day Model Patterns, and thus the trade entry techniques they best employ.

The day following a Persistent Trend Day Up might provide a short-sale entry if price provides some additional strength in the early going, but if a correction comes with the Open itself, or early in the 1st Frame action, a re-buy of that same Persistent Trend direction is often the next strategy at hand. And on the rare occasion two Persistent Trend Days do occur in the same trend direction back to back, a third day's follow-through has an extremely high probability of reversing that trend, either immediately or after an hour or two of follow-through.

■ Notes

1. George Douglass Taylor, *The Taylor Trading Technique* (Greenville, SC: Traders Press, 1950).
2. Linda Bradford Raschke, "Swing Trading: Rules and Philosophy," LBR Group, 2001. www.lbrgroup.com.

PART THREE

REPETITIVE CHART PATTERNS

What tales of timing the triangles tell,
the tell-tales told tag tails to the trends.

—Randolph Newman

Did not our bones and muscles contend against each other at every
turn, we could not rise or walk.

—Heraclitus

REPETITIVE CHART PATTERNS

CHAPTER 12

The Momentum Grid

As defined in an earlier chapter, a Split-Open Day Model signal tends to call price back to the ORB like a magnet. The problem for the Trader is how to identify when that process is ready again to occur. Loss of momentum is often an excellent gauge. Linda Bradford Raschke notes in her trading manual one of the key rules to technical analysis: momentum precedes price.[1] The Momentum Grid makes use of the comparison between stochastic momentum readings from two timeframes simultaneously, using the 1-minute and 10-minute time bars. Note the early Split-Open signal given in the NQ chart in Figure 12.1.

Price initially traded above, then below, back above, and then back to the ORB, as per rule definition. Later on toward the Noon Hour, several lows were testing lower price levels than initially achieved.

There are four elements to a valid entry signal using the Stochastic Grid tool, as seen in Figure 12.2. (For colorized versions of all the charts in this chapter, go to the Wiley companion website.) The pair of purple lines is created by a stochastic indicator calculated on a 10-minute time bar which is kept hidden from view to avoid distraction. The inputs for this stochastic setting are *Period D 7*, *Period K 14*, and *Smoothing 3*. The pair of green lines is created on 1-minute bars, also hidden. The inputs for the stochastic on the lower, 1-minute time frame bars are set to respond just slightly faster, with Period D 3, Period K 14 and Smoothing 3.[2]

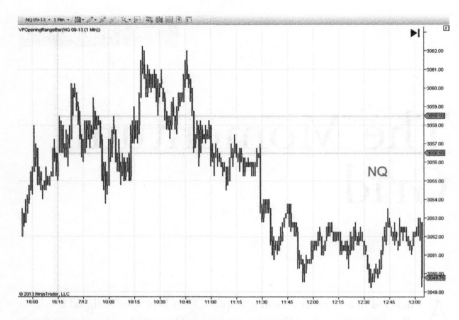

FIGURE 12.1 Price Expands the Range of a Split-Open Day Model

The elements of a signal we call the *Stochastic Split* begin first with the critical observation that the 10-minute stochastic has made the trip from an overbought reading near 90 to an oversold reading, just hooking under the number 10 on the graph by the faster moving of the pair, Period D, colored light purple. Both elements of this initial part to the signal are critical for the validation of the signal as a whole. The slower moving purple pair must make the trip from one extreme reading before breaching the opposite extreme reading, designated by the numbers 90 and 10 on the scale. The third element to the signal is that the lighter, faster of the 10-minute bar stochastic pair, in light purple, must cross back over the darker, slower of the pair, in dark purple. A few minutes later, the fourth and final element to this signal can occur. The green pair of stochastic lines that are calculated against the lower 1-minute time bars must make a trip of its own from the opposite extreme back to within the space created by the fresh crossover of the pair of 10-minute lines, filling that "split." See Figure 12.2.

The return of the 1-minute stochastic line to within the split of a turning 10-minute stochastic momentum indicator suggests that the retest of the nearby price extreme of the day will hold and turn the trend back towards the ORB, as in Figure 12.3.

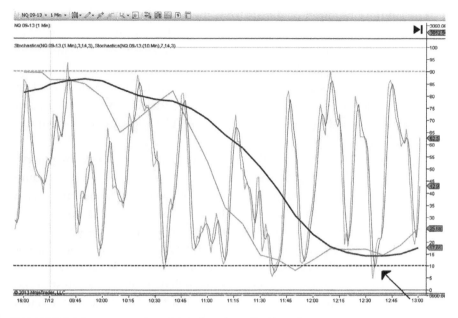

FIGURE 12.2 A Completed Stochastic Split Signal

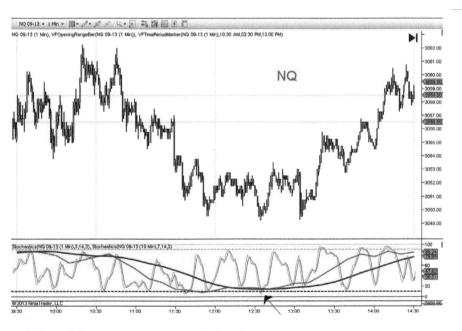

FIGURE 12.3 Momentum Turns before Price

The subtlety required of signals from the Momentum Grid is lost when compressing the indicator into a lower panel of the price bar chart, as in Figure 12.2. Therefore, the Momentum Grid should be kept in a window by itself, and occupying all the vertical scale a normal-sized computer screen has to offer. Monitors are inexpensive. I use six. One monitor can contain four Stochastic Grids, one for each of the four stock index instruments, in vertical panes, side-by-side, showing their complete vertical scale from top to bottom on the full screen.

The Test-and-Reject reversal opportunity can come in many forms. Sometimes price creates a more classic reversal pattern that may become recognizable as the end of the 1st Frame approaches. Sometimes price reverses immediately after accomplishing some parabolic price spike into a support or resistance zone, and mirrors on its trip back to the ORB in the pattern shape of the trend price made leaving it. For the latter, a measure of momentum is usually of little use, because momentum indicators are tools best used when gauging divergence, and as such need at least a retest of the nearby price extreme for comparison. And if a Test-and-Reject Day starts out with a large gap, such momentum indicators as those in the Stochastic Grid can accordingly be slammed against their own range extremes, arriving without having made the trip, and rendering their readings useless as a tool.

But like the action of the Split-Open Model, some 1st Trends of the Test-and-Reject Day accomplish a series of retests and noticeable changes in momentum readings that can serve as signals for the impending reversal, as in Figure 12.4.

Note in the example above how far this time the trend had already reversed before the StochSplit Signal was completed; and yet that small retracement bounce around 12:40 P.M. ET fit the signal for an entry that continued to produce a further downtrend excursion for several hours. And note too, that the green pair of stochastic lines are only required to reach the open split of the crossing purple 10-minute lines, wherever they are at the time, and do not require the green 1-minute lines to make a full trip back to the extreme grid readings. Often this target acquisition of the open space between the two 10-minute plots by the 1-minute stochastic does arrive coincidentally at a grid extreme, but that is not required of the signal.

And finally, that although the 1-minute stochastic lines may return to this rolling split area of the 10-minute stochastic lines several times, the signal for trade entry is only taken with any assurance of success on the initial

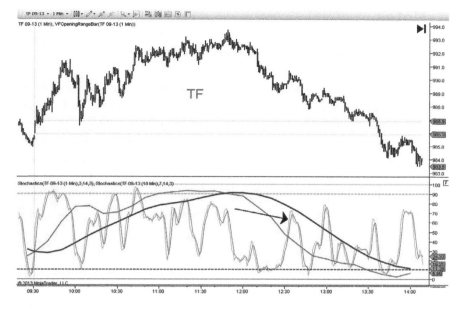

FIGURE 12.4 The StochSplit Signals a Later Entry Level

occurrence, as subsequent occurrences might come too late in the developing trend to risk such late entries.

The Persistent Trend Day Model does not produce working signals from this momentum indicator. On such days, momentum indicators continue to reflect extreme readings, and can even begin to roll over, all while price continues pushing on persistently into the prevailing trend.

■ Summary

Oscillators are notorious for their limitations. Making the trip from one extreme to the other is the first critical ingredient to a valid stochastic reversal signal. The StochSplit Signal is no exception and is therefore of far more use on Test-and-Reject and Split-Open Day Models than with the Persistent Trend. The signal is subtle and the study requires the presence of two timeframes on the same chart. Placing the pair of stochastic plots in a narrow panel at the bottom of the time bars will not leave enough space visually for the Trader to effectively monitor the appearance of this signal.

■ Notes

1. Linda Bradford Raschke, "Professional Trading Techniques," LBR Group, 1998. www.lbr.com.
2. The stochastic oscillator, invented by George Lane in the 1950s, is included as standard in most software chart packages, and can be programmed with the input preferences noted here. However, many chart packages do not allow two instances of this indicator calculated against different time frames to be superimposed into the same panel. NinjaCharts from Ninjatrader.com does allow this ability, and the ValhallaFutures Indicator Package, described in Appendix D, includes a template for quick installation of this configuration.

CHAPTER 13

Pre-Breakout Pause Pattern

The Test-and-Reject Model sometimes comes with a recognizable reversal pattern, but sometimes not. And even when it does, breakouts are fraught with the risk of whipsaw and early breakout failures. There is a very small and subtle price trigger that can form just prior to a breakout from a larger consolidation pattern. If taken as a trade entry device in conjunction with an incremental contract exit strategy, the risk for the overall position can be quite small.

Consolidation patterns by definition recognize an inability to trend. Some simply lack commitment and reflect a low open interest, and produce a tendency to drift. The pattern simply runs out of gas as price makes the trip from one end back to the other of its own range. But other patterns are more like coils. The range formed by the pattern in question has seemingly been built by a group of committed investors who have opened sizeable positions with breakout expectations, reflecting increased open interest, but to opposing trend outcomes. A *Pre-Breakout Pause Pattern* is simply a smaller gesture of the same price structure but in greater compression, and acts as a potential trigger to break free of the larger price consolidation.

Once the pattern in question is finally triggered, those traders positioned for a breakout at the other end of the pattern for the opposing trend outcome are stopped out. This stop-out level of those caught in the wrong direction can coincide with pressure of additional fresh entry orders from traders still on the sidelines who then want to participate in the direction of the fresh breakout. In addition, many of those being stopped out from the losing trend opinion then reenter a commitment—but now in the true breakout direction, stop-and-reverse, adding further to the heat of the newly emerging breakout trend.

A breakout that acts clean without choppy action into a sharp, fresh trend is not easy to predict. Once burned by breakouts that quickly fail, a trader can be reluctant to participate in this entry technique again. The presence of a small pause pattern however, usually in the form of a mini-channel or small pennant, can serve as a stepping-stone from which the breakout itself might find a base. When such a Pre-Breakout Pause Pattern appears, the risk is substantially reduced, and seems additionally to act as a signal that the breakout will, in fact, produce a considerable excursion.

This concept can be seen even in two charts of the preceding Chapter 12, if you now know what to look for. Sometimes, they arrive looking like a pattern within a pattern, as in Figure 13.1, taken from the same date and contract as Figure 12.4.

FIGURE 13.1 Pre-Breakout Pause as Pattern-within-Pattern

FIGURE 13.2 A Pre-Breakout Pause Sets Up above the Intraday Low

The same concept can also be seen in the graph of Figure 12.3 of Chapter 12, redrawn in close-up in Figure 13.2. Even though the Split-Open Signal suggests a trend away from the Opening Range Bar (ORB) will not get far, this Pre-Breakout Pause Pattern still provided a clean break for a short entry position.

These previous two examples were fairly obvious. The Trader trains his eye to look for them whenever a congestion pattern has occupied an entire 1st or Midday Frame. But the Pre-Breakout Pause setup is not always this elaborate. Of special note are the breakouts that can occur *without* the obvious presence of a Pre-Breakout Pause. If this becomes a necessary filter to using pattern breakout entries in the Trader's Trade Plan, some breakouts will naturally occur without his participation. But the charm of this pattern is that it can also appear just beyond the existing range of the larger consolidation pattern, instead of only within it. That is, the pause comes after an initial new price extreme is created without a prior pause pattern setup, as a kind of stutter-step. If so, an entry stop order can be used just beyond this *Post-Breakout Pause* in the same fashion. Sometimes this Post-Breakout Pause can occur with as simple a gesture as a single, 1-minute bar in the opposite direction to the eventual breakout, as in Figure 13.3.

FIGURE 13.3 Post-Breakout Pause Pattern Triggers a New Trend

Take note of further examples in the chapters that follow, as well as in the supplemental Wiley & Sons website for this book, with instructions in Appendix A.

■ Summary

Breakouts are fraught with failure. And nothing burns the Trader's fingers more than a position that fails within the first minute of entry following a false breakout. The Pre-Breakout Pause setup is no guarantee this won't happen, but when used with a Test-and-Reject Day Model, can greatly increase the chances to participate in the new trend without the potential whipsaw shakeout.

Think of it as a stepping-stone to the breakout. Its presence greatly increases the odds of success. Wise position management dictates a partial exit of at least one unit with the purpose of reducing the net risk to near break-even dollars shortly after the breakout occurs.

CHAPTER 14

The Classics Revisited

The New School of derivatives trading is the world of algorithms and data mining. Inherent to this pursuit is the belief that select participants are of some secret cognoscenti, and that by virtue of their business activities alone, trends begin and end in price. Track those in-the-know, anticipate them, recognize their footprints, and then beat them to the door if only by milliseconds of their arrival, and it will be you that rescues the narrow opportunity available from a game that is clearly fixed by these so otherwise specially advantaged.

Utter nonsense. And furthermore, the time and money that is being expended in the pursuit for faster Internet access and higher frequency trade execution—sometimes to the extremes of installing remote servers within the same physical proximity to those of the Chicago Mercantile Exchange (CME) itself—betrays a lack of understanding that the living market animal proceeds on its own pace as it fleshes out trend and trend reversal pattern, independent of how quickly the participants actually arrive at the gates.

Lost in all this flutter over faster exchange server access is the acknowledgment that no amount of speed improvement or higher frequency trading volume will push a lazy consolidation pattern that's forming throughout the 1st Frame of the day any sooner toward its eventual fruition. High frequency trading and algorithmic data analysis has been hard at work for many years now, but just look at the many classic chart patterns formed within the Test-and-Reject Models taken from the current contract expiration months at the time of this book, mid-2013. All that was needed for this author to make screen captures of the *trade frequency* to these patterns was a quick perusal of a few weeks preceding this book's publisher editorial deadlines. Nor do you need to locate your trade platform PC on a server located within the block of the CME on South Wacker Drive. Instead, let's take a walk back to Old School.

■ M-Tops, W-Bottoms

If Test-and-Reject is the most common behavior model of the daily trend, then understanding its more typical forms will lend the Trader great decision support for entries. Chart pattern recognition is all that is needed to capitalize on the potential contained on many a Test-and-Reject Day setups, where many of the classic chart patterns well known but apparently long forgotten exhibit 'high frequency' reappearance.

Focus for a moment on Figure 14.1. Note how we've included the previous day's action that reveals the previous Persistent Trend Day Down and— to provide further background to the day that followed—reveal that the larger weekly frame trend of the market during this period of 2013 was in a relentless bull trend (not shown).

FIGURE 14.1   W-Bottom of a Test-and-Reject

A good deal of the expected cycle correction to the Persistent Trend Day had been accomplished by the very large gap-up opening. Some backward action to absorb this gap was hardly unexpected. But whether it took the form of a 1st Frame triangle, *W-Bottom*, or inverse *Head-and-Shoulders* was less important than the simple understanding that if the 1st Frame was consumed in consolidation, the Midday Frame would produce the trend, *yang-yin*. In no way did high frequency trading or millisecond speed improvements to execution have anything to do with the recognition or subsequent execution of trade entries based on these pattern models. The small Post-Breakout Pause Pattern that appeared in the W-Bottom of Figure 14.1, which was depicted in the close-up of Figure 13.3 from Chapter 13, did, however, have a great deal to do with a trade entry. Who needed a Chicago server address for that?

An M-Top is simply the bear version of the W-Bottom, just as the inverse Head-and-Shoulders pattern the bull version of the bearish Head-and-Shoulders top. (For further examples, see the Wiley companion website for this book—instructions in Appendix A.)

■ Telltale Triangles

The 1st Frame triangles can be tricky to trade. They are often imprecise. One set of perceived trend lines gives away to another, only to broaden and further extend the formation of the triangle pattern in time and price. False breakouts therefore abound. The construct is eye-of-the-beholder. In fact, the pattern in Figure 14.1 could have as easily been depicted a triangle as the W-Bottom identity given it. The Trader doesn't care. He's aware that the previous day's Persistent Trend Day Down has been reversed by a strong opening. He sees that no fresh lower lows have occurred by the 10:30 A.M. Trend Check. He's watching the shot clock run out on the 1st Frame, which has been entirely contained by consolidation. The dichotomy is simple. If it can't go down to close that opening gap, and it's unlikely to go sideways throughout another whole frame, it's going to seek the price levels that most facilitate new trading. If it can't go down, it's going up. The strategy is then to position buy-stops for a potential bull breakout.

In general, triangles that spend the greater of the 1st Frame in formation on one side of the ORB tend to breakout to the opposite side. See Figure 14.2.

FIGURE 14.2 TF 1st Frame Triangle, Test-and-Reject

If the triangle is large and volatile enough, it may extend its formation well into the Midday Frame before reaching fruition, and is therefore not exclusive to 1st Frame action, as in Figure 14.3.

Note the small Pre- and Post-Breakout Pause Patterns associated with the successful lower red trend line break. Note too, how the triangle seems to have redrawn itself from another trend line higher up. This is typical triangle behavior and must be tolerated if not employed. A return-to-the-broken-trend line is also very atypical triangle behavior. Usually, trailing a stop-loss level on a "runner" must be curtailed until a trend line retest is firmly behind the action of the developing trend breakout.

Rather than being the end of a trend, triangles often appear just *before* the end of a trend, and therefore presage an even bigger reversal looming somewhere out in space and time to the right of the video screen. This trend will often then come back to and through the original triangle breakdown. That bigger picture means little to the intraday trader who captured the initial breakout trend with a trailing stop-loss order anyway. The presence of a triangle in the 1st Frame should always open the possibility that the

FIGURE 14.3 A Midday Frame Triangle

Test-and-Reject concept could occur at both ends of a day's whole trading range, still with the purpose of uncovering a final and truer trend in the larger timeframe, as in Figure 14.4.

So much of typical triangle behavior is told in the story of this graph in Figure 14.4. Consider that action as described in the following list:

- The triangle punctuates the cycle rotation of Day Models. The large 1st Frame triangle of June 6, 2013 appeared the day after the Persistent Trend Day Down of June 5, suggesting at some point, price would reverse back up.

- An upside breakout of that same triangle seems to have precluded the eventual bear move down. No clear Pre-Breakout Pause Pattern developed before that false bull breakout. As a rule, a false breakout in one direction of a triangle encourages a successful breakout on the other side. Nothing begets the success of a 2nd trend down like the failure to initiate a 1st trend up. This particular triangle behavior is just one of the reasons trading triangles can be so frustrating to the less-experienced trader.

- The 1st Frame Triangle breakdown was a presage to the end of the bear trend. The "tell-tales told tag tails to the trends," as my mentor Randolph Newman use to quip. (See the complete quote at the beginning of Part Three.)

FIGURE 14.4 Ending Triangles

- The bear breakdown trend ends in another triangle, mirroring in reverse what proceeded just before. This elicits another typical triangle behaviorism: A pair of triangles tends to call the end of a trend.

- Price is checked on the way back up by the apex of the 1st Frame triangle. The apex of the triangle can be considered unfinished business. If the reversal back into the triangle is strong, the apex won't check price for long. But the Trader who is aware of this price level can exit most or all positions against it, or use tighter stop-loss positioning as it approaches, and then consider reentering if price can successfully get past the triangle apex altogether.

The millennium bull market in technology stocks ended in the year 2000 with the formation of a huge triangle in the Nasdaq 100 Index. The largest ending triangle of all time appeared between 1921 and 1926 in the Axe-Houghton Industrial Stock Price Average, setting up the huge final rally that culminated in the historic, pre-crash stock market top of September–October 1929.[1] Just before Apple Computer reached its current all-time high of 705 in September of 2012, a triangle appeared that consumed its pre-top price action from April to August of that same year. And the last price pattern appearing before the 2012 gold bull began losing so much of its recent 2013 luster was—you guessed it—a triangle. "What tales of timing the triangles tell."

■ Head-and-Shoulders Reversals, Revised

This pattern is typically favored by the majority of new traders. It is the most easily recognized and most often looked for. That alone makes it subject to the most suspicion and least consistency of performance. But the experienced Trader is far more accustomed to the Head-and-Shoulders (H&S) pattern failure; so much so that is usually a far better exercise to consider the possibilities of a continuation of the prevailing trend than as the reversal action a Head-and-Shoulders breakout is so often reputed to produce. If price can't or won't go the one expected reversal direction, chances are high it deceives the majority and proceeds on in the opposite.

But there is one feature that tends to confirm that an appearance of this classic pattern may, in fact, be true. Instead of placing all one's focus on the usual price level of the *neckline*, study instead the price level being formed by the shoulders. Whether in a potential H&S Top pattern, or its inverse formation as a bottom, the rightmost shoulder should not be closer to the price extreme of the head than is the left. The rightmost shoulder can be the same or greater distance from the most extreme price level of the head, but if in fact it's closer to the head, consider filtering this setup out as a trade entry reversal because that H&S pattern is far more likely to fail.

Nearly everyone in the ValhallaFutures chat room pointed out the potential inverse Head-and-Shoulders bottom pattern on the day the one appeared in Figure 14.5.

In this example, the right shoulder dipped lower than the left, and as an added signal to a possible trend-continuation position, a Pre-Breakdown Pause Pattern appeared as an order entry trigger with which to capitalize on this classic pattern's potential failure.

The failure of a reversal pattern in the expected direction is usually a valid signal for continuation of the trend. The bigger the H&S setup, the better the failure reaction to the otherwise expected direction. From this we can add a second corollary to the initial Douglas Premise.

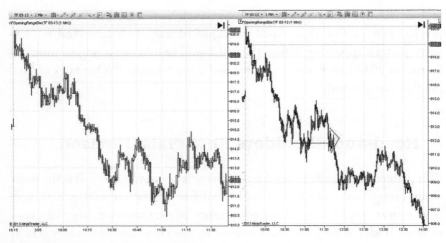

FIGURE 14.5 TF before and after an inverse H&S Setup

Corollary #2 to the Douglas Premise

If most of the money lost in the markets is lost by traders who thought they knew which way the market was supposed to go, then most of the opportunity missed in the markets is missed by traders who couldn't concede that the market might go the expected distance, but in the opposite direction.

When the H&S pattern does conform to this new rule regarding the smaller right shoulder, a subsequent reversal breakout tends to at least reach a *Measured Move* target, regardless of whether the broken neckline was leaning into or away from the direction of the subsequent breakout, as in Figure 14.6.

To demonstrate this concept in ideal laboratory conditions, we'd find two comparable financial instruments trading within the same day's market conditions, and watch them both create potential tops in the shape of the classic Head-and-Shoulders reversal pattern; one that conforms to the rule of the right shoulder remaining smaller than the left, and the other violating this rule, as in Figure 14.7, both from July 1, 2013, both showing the Close.

If the angle of the neckline itself were the proper qualifying criteria, the TF chart on the right of Figure 14.7 would seem the better choice. And it could be fairly said that the TF's neckline break did at least allow the Trader enough cushion of profit to reach a net break-even stop-loss risk using a two-unit strategy. But the truly successful trade was a short in the ES, whose right shoulder, unlike the TF's, was clearly smaller than its left.

FIGURE 14.6 H&S Shoulder, Neckline, and Target Considerations

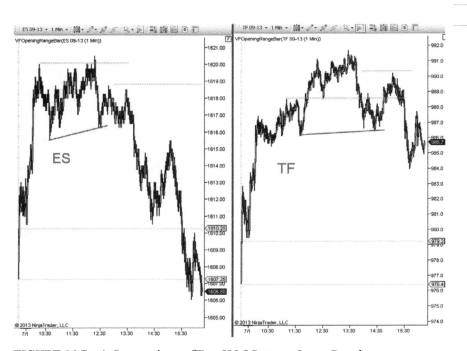

FIGURE 14.7 A Comparison of Two H&S Pattern Setup Results

■ The Rising/Declining Wedge

The Diagonal Triangle, or wedge formation, is one of the most consistent reversal patterns on the board. Look for it after a Persistent Trend Day, especially where price opens near the previous day's Close and then continues in the direction of the previous day's trend. Since a correction on that day of the Day Model Sequence Cycle is more likely, chances improve that a break of the inside trend line will signal a good reversal, as in Figure 14.8, the same graph was used in Chapter 9, Figure 9.1, for the Test-and-Reject Model. (A colorized version is available on the Wiley companion website.)

Note the brief Pre-Breakout Pause Pattern that developed just before the break. The bear correction to this pattern came in a single sharp spike. The usual target for such a pattern is just the base of the wedge pattern itself. This correction carried all the way down to fill an open gap from the day before, Work-Done.

A temptation might arise to use such a sharp break as a signal that a correction of larger degree might have begun. But in the 3–5 day cycle, the correction day can easily become the Buy Day of the next cycle. Anyone carrying overnight a short position from that break as a swing trade in the daily timeframe would have been sorely disappointed, as can be seen

REPETITIVE CHART PATTERNS

FIGURE 14.8 A Rising Wedge Triggers a Short-Term Reversal

FIGURE 14.9 Two 3-Day Cycles, with the 2nd Enlarged

in the opening price of the next day. This is one of the reasons we remain focused on strategies for intraday swings, and refrain from holding positions overnight. A weak close does not necessarily mean a weak opening on the following day, as any close examination of the Taylor 3-Day Cycle will reveal.

As consistent as the Rising Wedge is as a reversal pattern, it is not without its counterpart in trend outcome. Again, always consider the context of the Day Model Sequence. On the left of the chart in Figure 14.9, two 3-Day Cycles have been compressed into 5-minute time bars for easier viewing. The chart on the right is a selected enlargement of one on the left, and examines the beginning of the second of those two Taylor cycles. (For a colorized version, see the Wiley companion website.)

Note the first Rising Wedge in the leftmost pane comes as the Test-and-Reject reversal pattern following a Persistent Trend Day Up (similar but not identical to the one depicted in Figure 14.8). The second Rising Wedge depicted in Figure 14.9 was another day removed from the first one, and therefore, not immediately following a Persistent Trend Day Up.

The pane on the right is simply an enlargement of that second Rising Wedge pattern. Study how it differs from the one the day before. If considered on its own without the strong context of the 3-Day Cycle, and for its obvious resemblance to the Rising Wedge Reversal pattern, many traders would no doubt see it as a short-sale opportunity, expecting yet another bear breakdown like the day before. But the underlying trend and the cycle rotation was a more dominant issue than the expected outcome to this classic pattern. No doubt, had the pattern been a Head-and-Shoulders Top formation instead of that second Rising Wedge, it too would have failed as a reversal, and triggered as a continuation pattern back into the bull cycle as well.

When price breaks out from this pattern not as a reversal but instead in the same direction as the angle of the classic *Rising/Declining Wedge*, the pattern is called a *Running Correction*. This version of the wedge is actually a continuation pattern, not a reversal, and can also appear within the middle of a Persistent Trend Day, where a reversal is also typically anticipated somewhere in the Midday Frame, but does not arrive. Again, it's the underlying trend and the rotation of the 3-Day Cycle that is predominant, not the Trader's expectations or the textbook interpretation of these well-known patterns. "The scholar most in repute knows only what is reputed," as Heraclitus so wisely observed.

■ Midday Channel

Another continuation pattern associated with the middle of a Persistent Trend Day or the 2nd Trend of a Test-and-Reject Day is the Midday Channel. In the middle of the day, a congestion period often occurs that has a sideways direction. This pattern model often frustrates traders because it is associated with false breakouts and faux reversals. The beauty of the pattern on trending days is that it usually sets up about halfway between the range extremes of the day, providing a Measured Move target once a true breakout has triggered. It does require some patience to let the pattern take shape, along with an understanding as to how the model usually triggers.

Note the telltale pattern characteristics that are described along with the series of charts that follow. The *Midday Channel* is best understood in stages. The early *tell* to a budding Midday Channel is the repeated attempt at reversing the trend with a number of small countertrend thrusts that end in approximately—but almost never exactly—the same price point. The "never exactly" at the same price is an important part of the pattern's tell. If, on the other hand, price reversals are checked by exactly the same price number, an eventual breakout of that price level will more likely make the reversal successful. A true channel is, therefore, more likely to be disguised

FIGURE 14.10 A Channel Might Be Forming

by an irregular range, making slightly lower lows or higher highs as it drifts onward. To counter this, draw a perfectly horizontal line, only approximating the inside channel boundary where the reversal attempts have failed, as in Figure 14.10.

When this pattern forms, the end of the 1st Frame has usually come and gone. An extended move like this usually sets up the *possibility* of a reversal. At this point, this far into a trend, it is hard to imagine there could be significantly more of the same trend distance covered without a reversal. Such a mindset, which makes it difficult to concede that price could continue a further, significant distance without a reversal to the trend, is all part of this pattern's tell.

At this point, the exercise of analysis regarding this pattern is still just building the possible argument for a Midday Channel. Finish prescribing the channel now by drawing the outer boundary line, again perfectly horizontal, averaging the trend's current extreme by ignoring a tick or two of one or more of the furthest price extremes. Then, move the current channel to the middle of your computer screen by increasing the vertical scale. Concede that anything is possible. The result of repeated failures to reverse could have consequence at any time. And remember this excerpt from Corollary #2 to the Douglas Premise, "most of the opportunity missed in the markets is missed by traders who couldn't concede...."

Without a Pre-Break Pause, a further breakdown will be suspect. But if any Pre-Break Pause appears, as in Figure 14.11, be willing to enter a position in the direction of the trend using a stop-entry order just beyond any pause in the 1-minute bar frame.

Once triggered, the *Channel Center Line* measures a move halfway from the day's earliest price toward the pattern's expected target, as in Figure 14.12.

The Center Line is a key element to the Midday Channel. Sometimes price will return after a successful breakout and test the Center Line before continuing on to its measured target. This may cause the Trader a stop-out of any remaining position runners. Unless the target has already been met, be prepared to reenter the position at the Center Line should this occur. The protective stop for such an entry is a few ticks beyond the far side of the channel that the Center Line dissects.

FIGURE 14.11 A Pre-Breakout Pause Appears

FIGURE 14.12 Price Reaches the Target by the End-of-Day

Since the channel often forms as a continuation pattern within a Persistent Trend Day, price will usually reverse on the following day back to the channel. If there's enough time left, and the Measured Move target following the channel breakout has been met, price might even make it back to the channel on the same day. The Center Line may repel the initial advance, but once beyond that level, a larger reversal is probable, especially if that reversal is part of a return to the underlying trend of the daily/weekly timeframe and the 3-Day Cycle.

Further examples of these pattern concepts can also be found on the Wiley companion website for this book. See the instructions in Appendix A.

■ Summary

No discoveries of complex algorithms or improvements in speed to execution seem to have any effect whatsoever on the repetitive patterns of human behavior. The same footprints from the usual suspects of pattern formation continue to show up regardless. Classic reversal patterns often show up in the Test-and-Reject model, and those that periodically fail, such as the H&S and Wedge, can appear as effective to trend continuation for profit opportunity as the distance expected by their traditional reversals. If given the right signals, concede that the market can as easily go the expected distance, but in the opposite direction. Trend prejudice is a killer to understanding opportunity and capturing profits. Be the Trader. The Trader takes action on models that appear at the right edge of his video screen regardless of which way the market is supposed to go.

■ Note

1. See Appendix E.

CHAPTER 15

MA Pattern Concepts

Moving averages aren't normally thought of as patterns. Mostly they're used to derive entry signals based on the crossover of a faster moving average through a slower. In this text, the 89 and 200 Exponential Moving Averages in the 1-minute bar frame have been described for their use as dynamic short-term exhaustions levels, components of our overall Pivot/ Exhaustion Grid. As a crossover signal system, they would be far too slow and lagging. Instead, their plots should be thought of as a sort of trampoline net to pricing, giving way to a sudden price spike, but bouncing right back with the enthusiasm of a spring, at least until the trend is ready to reverse altogether.

Trends do change direction. A 2nd Persistent Trend Day Model occurring on the heels of one in the same direction will not behave like the first. And if the Trader can learn to observe the price action around, through, and between the 89 and 200EMAs, a number of trend signals can contribute to Trade Entry Models at this battle ground and crossroad of trend outcome.

◼ The EMA Pinch

As discussed in Part Two, "Day Model Patterns," the 200EMA exhaustion zone is best represented by the action on a Persistent Trend Day. On that day, these two EMAs, the 89 and 200, are usually well out of play until well after the 1st Frame, as price slows it advances and allows the look-back window of the moving average calculation to play catch-up. As price momentum wanes, the EMA line plots inch closer to the slowing action. Even before the Persistent Trend has run its length in the 1st Frame sprint, an initial pullback to the 89EMA occasionally offers an in-trend entry. But it's not until later, after the momentum of the Persistent Trend has waned, usually late in the Midday Frame or early in Last Hour Time Frame, that the long awaited Last Chance Texaco correction presents itself. Slowly rolling the trend backward at first, this correction can gather a sudden burst of momentum, and present itself as if a solid reversal trend, spiking through the 200EMA.

As per our Corollary #1 to the Douglas Premise, "most of the money to be made in the market is made at the places where most traders are proven wrong and stopped-out." As long as this is not the 2nd Persistent Trend Day model in a row of the short-term cycle, this 200EMA spike usually creates a kind of double whammy of stop-outs. The in-trend position holders trying to stay with runners have trailed stop-loss orders to just behind nearby pullbacks pivots, leaving those orders vulnerable to this Midday Frame correction. Countertrend traders, having eyed a plethora of extreme indicator readings for the Persistent Trend, enter new positions in the direction of the accelerating pullback instead of the trend, as if the long-awaited reversal had finally begun. The sharp acceleration of momentum on the break of the 200EMA certainly appears to be supporting evidence that a reversal is just beginning. But this one, larger countertrend move to the Persistent Trend Day often ends with a vertical spike just where it seems to have gathered the most speed. Sometimes a Die Bar is also present. If these reversal traders are now proven wrong, their stop-loss orders will only add to the fire that brings price action back solidly in the direction of the Persistent Trend.

Unfortunately, it is difficult to gauge how far price will spike on that initial break through the 200EMA. Sometimes it's only a tick or two. Sometimes it feeds on the stop-loss orders it's running, plus the add-on orders coming into the market by those thinking the much-awaited correction has finally begun. A sharp thrust through this 200EMA will usually deliver a sense of fear into the hearts of traders, and entering an order against this spike, back in the direction of the Persistent Trend will often seem like catching the proverbial knife.

If the 89 and 200EMAs have already crossed over as this reversal spike appears, chances are that even after a bounce back up, the trend is indeed in trouble. But a Persistent Trend Day will almost never lead with such a crossover first, and instead, the EMAs may only be closing into a narrowing channel, more like a pair of railroad rails than at the angle necessary to make a crossover, as in Figure 15.1.

FIGURE 15.1 The Pinch of the EMAs

As can be seen, price action reverses sharply back from the trampoline-like buoyancy of the 200EMA. It's as if price is aware of the closing space between the 89 and 200EMA line plots, fearful it won't get through the closing doors in time to recapture the Persistent Trend. The appearance of this pinch can come on any day's correction, and does not necessarily have to be associated with only the Persistent Trend.

In truth, during a Persistent Trend Day, price can be so eager to get back into trend after it clips the 200EMA that it never actually has time to pinch anyway. A closer look at the reversal action just prior to reaching the Pinch in Figure 15.1 reveals a small flag had formed as a Pre-Breakout Pause Pattern, serving as another chance to enter the trade long, had the 2:30 P.M. Transition Time not been more precisely utilized.

▌ Gap-Close . . . or Further?

On the day following a Persistent Trend day, price will often gap away from that yesterday's Close to open sharply into the direction of that previous day's trend. But as discussed in the section on Day Model Sequence Cycle, this gap is prone

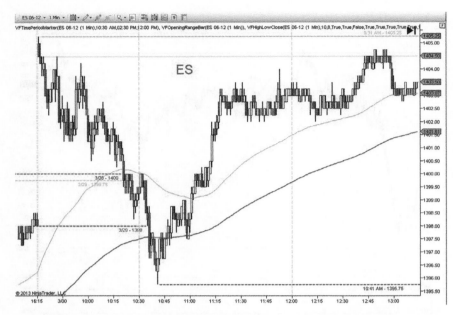

FIGURE 15.2 A Trampoline Bounce from the 200EMA, Test-and-Reject

to reverse, even if the day starts off as a gap-n-go initially. Once a reversal is in place, and a gap closing is in the sites of a budding Test-and-Reject Day Model reversal, price often gains momentum, and can run right through the Y-Close gap level, as if it meant nothing at all. On such days as this, a spike past the gap-close and through the lagging 200EMA can be the best signal that the reversal has run its course. And even if price develops further into the reversal trend later in the morning, that initial break of the 200EMA, after having made such a vertical trip to get there, usually provides a very profitable bounce. (See Figure 15.2.)

■ The EMA Cup

The importance to further EMA trend signals comes from how price behaves from in between the 89 and 200EMAs on the 1-minute bars—a place we call the *EMA Cup*, when price makes the trip back to this area after a period of vacation. No trend will forever be contained by the 200EMA. Trends change in the larger frame, and the EMAs must cross over at some point to reflect that change. Even then, making the trip to and slightly through the 200EMA usually produces exhaustion.

The focus on whether the 200EMA is really going to work for its trampoline-like bounce back into the previous trend gets its closest scrutiny on a day after a Persistent Trend Day, when action has continued in a follow-through to the

Persistent Trend Day's direction. It's on this day after that price is far more likely to reverse. And when the trend is really changing, price will often be *cupped* by the EMAs, especially if the EMA pair is not really pinching at that point. And if that level succeeds in containing the bounce from the trampoline-like action of the elastic 200EMA, that 200EMA may be tested again and subsequently be broken. A second break of the 200EMA after price has been contained by the EMA Cup usually means the trend is in the process of changing, and the correction itself is becoming the new trend. Study Figure 15.3.

Note too, how price behaves just as these two EMAs finally cross. Although the full crossover may be an indication that the trend is in the process of change, the exact occurrence of the crossover itself usually comes precisely at a point of short term exhaustion to the new trend change. This is typical 89–200EMA crossover behavior. As such, the crossover of these two EMAs is rarely an actual entry trigger. When it is a signal to get it, the overall price pattern is not one of a sharp correction or vertical spike of price crashing down into and through the 200EMA. The rare times the 89–200EMA crossover *is* an entry signal comes when price has been going sideways for an extended period through the Midday Frame without volatility, and as a roll out from

FIGURE 15.3 The Cup Contains the 200EMA Spike Reversal

this extended consolidation pattern, breaks through support forcing the 89 to cross over the 200EMA at about the same time as the breakout itself, and often near the 2:30 P.M. Transition Time.

This warning regarding the crossover concept deserves this emphasis here because so many traders have been trained in using EMA crossover systems for trade entry. As stated earlier, the 89 and 200EMAs, as plotted in the 1-minute bar frame, are not good candidates for such a system in volatile reversal action.

■ The Cup as Breakout Trigger

On some days, a Test-and-Reject Day Model may build its reversal pattern right on top of the 89 and 200EMAs, just as if to tempt the fate of their properties of support/resistance. Watch for the Cup to actually frame the Pre-Breakout Pause Pattern to the larger reversal, as seen in the M-Top Reversal Pattern of Figure 15.4.

FIGURE 15.4 The Cup as Pre-Breakout Pause

■ Summary

If price has been crisscrossing the 89 and 200EMAs repeatedly during a day or two of trading, expect the reactions to grow increasingly meaningless. That would indicate a trading range. In contrast, it's the trip back to the 200EMA after an extensive move away from it that lends to it that trampoline-style price rejection to a penetrating spike.

Thereafter, watch for the EMA Cup. If the 89EMA contains the reversal from the 200, chances are higher that a true change of trend is at hand and a further break of the 200EMA is imminent. The whole issue of whether further price breaks beyond the 200EMA becomes a trend of its own can often be cued from the Day Model Sequence Cycle. Remember, the market very rarely ever makes two Persistent Trend Days a row in the same direction without an extensive correction to that trend.

PART FOUR

CONFLUENCE AND EXECUTION

I'd rather be sorry than safe.

—Randolph Newman

They do not grasp how being at variance it agrees with itself.

—Heraclitus

CHAPTER 16

Transition Time Reversals

In Chapter 1, "A Three-Frame Day," I introduced the broad concept of a day split into three time periods, or frames. The message told the importance of establishing a kind of cadence to the ebb and flow of the day. Consolidation shifts to trend, volatility shifts back to drift, action is countered by reaction. On most days, this is simply how the market behaves. Certain Persistent Trend Day behavior is the only real exception. Since the market can never become too predictable, this whole concept can be categorized as a generality, but it remains nonetheless an observable phenomenon that the static Transition Time Markers are often the focus of change in price action or trend.

The 12 P.M. Transition Time was only mentioned briefly in Chapter 1 as a member of the Time Marker set. Of this set, these four are worth monitoring for their contribution to price position: the 10:30 A.M. Trend Check, the 11:15 A.M. Transition Time, the Noon Hour Transition Time (also see brief discussion of the Noon Hour High/Low in Chapter 6), and the 2:30 P.M. Transition Time. (All times referenced remain Eastern Standard.)

Outside of the observable behavior of Time Markers in the charts, there is no reason or rhyme why they should have any affect whatsoever on the market at all as potential pivots. The Trader doesn't care about logic. He lets the markets do all the talking. Like most all of the other concepts in this book, with perhaps the exception of the ORB Breakout Patterns, none are used solely on their own to enter a trade. But the contribution these static Time Markers lend to the daily trend picture as a whole can become the

FIGURE 16.1 Time Markers and Price Swings

critical missing element to the confluence of signals we call a Trade Entry Model.

So let the charts speak. In Figure 16.1, note the cadence the Time Markers bring to the major price swings of the day.

First, price reverses at the 10:30 Trend Check and then tests the ORB. The Noon Hour comes as the right shoulder of a large potential M-Top reversal pattern. When such a pattern triggers, as did this one, it sponsors a breakdown of the ORB into a Test-and-Reject pattern for the day. On the day in Figure 16.1, the trend continued downward toward a 2:30 Transition Time low. An understanding of the intersection of these key technical parts can give the Trader an opportunity to take advantage of the whole, and target exits and entries around the confluence of these technical events.

We don't look for price necessarily making a new 1st Frame high or low at the 10:30 Trend Check, as this time is notorious for appearing as a pullback before continuing on into the same trend. The ES and NQ contracts in Figure 16.2 are from different days, but demonstrate the timing of a typical 10:30 pullback.

The 10:30 Trend Check can also be associated with aiding breakouts as well as reversals and pullbacks. Figure 16.3 depicts a Test-and-Reject reversal pattern on the cusp of a breakout.

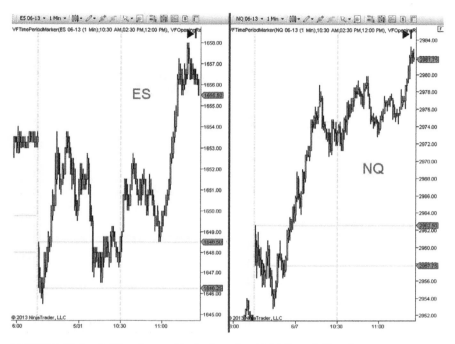

FIGURE 16.2 Pullbacks are Typical at the 10:30 Trend Check

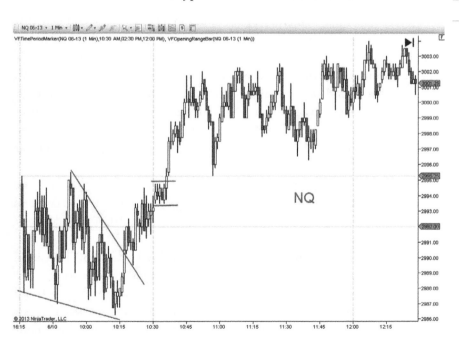

FIGURE 16.3 A Breakout Triggers at the 10:30 Trend Check

FIGURE 16.4 Persistent Trend with a 10:30 Pre–Breakout Pause

Figure 16.4 displays an entry opportunity in a Persistent Trend Day that employs the same device as that depicted in Figure 16.3.

The Noon Hour is most often associated with a new daily high or daily low. Breakouts or further trend extensions that appear at Noon tend to suffer pullbacks and occasionally reverse altogether from that point for the rest of the day. But although a Noon Hour reversal can be fairly precise, it is always temporary on the Persistent Trend Day, and usually temporary if occurring during the 2nd Trend of a Test-and-Reject Day, just as in Figure 16.5.

Regardless of the norm, the Noon Hour is really just another Time Marker. Less common but just as effective, the Noon Hour can also come as a pullback to the ongoing trend, in the same way as the 10:30 Trend Check more often does, as in Figure 16.6.

As displayed in so many of the charts in this book, the 2:30 Transition Time is most consistent reversal time of the four Time Markers. The charts in Figure 16.5 display another example. But like the 10:30 Trend Check, the 2:30 Transition Time can—when arriving on a very late reversal to the Test-and-Reject Day—trigger a breakout into an extended last hour trend, as in Figure 16.7.

FIGURE 16.5 Noon Hour Low, Precise but Temporary

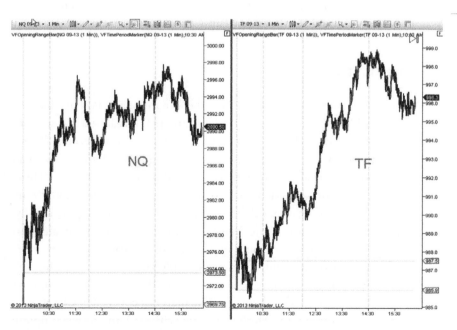

FIGURE 16.6 Noon Hour Pullbacks to the Ongoing Trend

FIGURE 16.7   A Pre-Breakout Pause at the 2:30 Transition Time

A trend pivot at the 2:30 Transition Time is so consistent that it can't decide whether it earns the nickname "2:30 Trend Trigger" or just plain "Trend Killer." Watch for reversals and Pre-Breakout Pause Patterns at this time of day.

■ Summary

The existence of Transition Time Markers defies a rationale. Perhaps like the concept of the Floor Trader's Pivots, traders anticipate a reaction and so react in anticipation. We care about results, and so it makes no difference. Think of the day's trend swings being punctuated by these Time Markers. Keep an open, unprejudiced mind as to how or where in the charts they arrive. These Time Markers are not necessarily precise as to price pivot, and should only be considered in terms of what other trading patterns are developing nearby.

On any given day, these Time Markers will mean nothing at all. And therein is the rub. When something doesn't seem to work for a few days, the less-disciplined trader will begin to let slide the habit of plotting the necessary vertical line markers, and soon some of the best decision support of the day will go unnoticed and unused. The material covered in Chapter 17 demonstrates how these Time Markers can be critical elements to complete a Technical Trade Entry Model.

Trade Entry Models

The Trader must commit his funds at the right edge of the video screen. He cannot look ahead without suffering the prejudices of prediction, and he cannot look back very far before the opportunity has already come and gone. Thus, in order to reduce risk and limit his commitments only to those trades that stand the best chances, he defines a Trade Entry Model around a confluence of disparate technical market elements, which taken together might signal a trend continuation or reversal for the whole. This chapter is meant to bring together the various technical concepts explored in earlier chapters into that whole.

Many students who seek mentoring often reveal in initial conversations that they only monitor the one stock index futures contract they are actually trading. It's as if they expected their trading to improve by this singular focus. As regarding the additional effort, my experience in mentoring so many hundreds of traders over the years is that some are only too ready to dismiss as irrelevant something they would rather simply avoid expending the energy on to include. But even in the smaller intraday frames, the market will only complete a trend or pullback if most of the stocks that make up the market are willing to turn as well. The Dow, the NASDAQ and the Russell 2000 all focus on different segments of the market. The successful identity of an Entry Model requires a confluence of disparate technical events that involve the whole market in order to trigger the business of fresh trend continuance or reversal.

The concept of a *Technical Event Model* then becomes a little more complex and a lot more meaningful when trend and technical accomplishments arrive simultaneously between two different index contracts. As per the lessons in this book, there are a variety of technical accomplishments that can influence trend reversal and trend extension. Some are based on price intersections with support and resistance we call a Pivot/Exhaustion Grid; some are based on Moving Average price exhaustion; some technical accomplishments are based on pattern fruition; some on momentum decline; some are based on static time cycles throughout the day we call Transition Times; and some technical aspects are based on cycles that are present in the larger daily frame, like Taylor's 3-Day Cycle and the rotation sequence of Day Models.

This is hardly an exhaustive list. Although I have, for the most part, dismissed Fibonacci studies for Event Entry Model considerations, far better traders and scholars of greater repute swear by its significance. I do accept the premise that there is an internal structure to the market based on the repetitive nature of human behavior when acting in mass and making mass decisions about it. If there were not, familiar classic chart patterns would never so often reappear. Chaos structure found in wave theory, therefore, should also merit inclusion. Just because the eye doesn't immediately recognize some chaos fractals doesn't mean they don't repeat themselves throughout the short-term trend cycle of trend to correction on a daily basis.

As for the application of Elliott Wave Theory to such fractal structures, I was unable, after many years of both study and practice, to find consistent decision support from Elliott Wave methods applied in the lower time frames. And it was simply beyond the scope of this book to include my own contribution to wave analysis with that of the Serial Sequent Wave Method™, as it requires software to calculate the necessary algorithms and label the fractal segments of chaos structure into the trend reversal and breakout signals it elicits so remarkably. Students seeking to delve further into that groundbreaking work can read about it in Appendix C. But suffice it to say that there are many consistently successful traders in the marketplace who have never even heard of it, and would have no need to include it in the successful Trade Plans they already employ.

Instead, I have chosen to represent as elements of potential Trade Entry Models the kind of technical trend events easily observed in the action of the smaller time frames where the intraday trader resides, and by means of simple tools available to students in such free, downloadable software charting packages as from NinjaTrader.com. And despite the breadth of market participation required to view these technical events simultaneously, the

FIGURE 17.1   ES, NQ Reach Disparate Support Levels

understanding and application of their confluence is terribly simple. This has been Old School thinking.

With an understanding of the concepts introduced so far in this book, consider the simplicity of the message contained in Figure 17.1. (Colorized versions of all figures in Chapter 17 are available on the Wiley companion website.)

Note in Figure 17.1 how the NQ was leading the market down toward the end of the 1st Hour, making a new low for the day. The student has now learned from countless examples in this book how a fresh intraday low is not necessarily a confirmation of a downtrend, but far more likely to suggest trend exhaustion in the intraday frame. In the process, the NQ was also closing the gap left open from the previous day.

Now note the ES. Keep in mind that index comprises 500 of the largest capitalized stocks on the NYSE, and alongside the high-tech glamour names of the NASDAQ, represent a huge portion of the total market. Near the 10:30 A.M. Trend Check, at the moment the NQ was closing its gap, the ES was returning to the Opening Range, an important level of support/resistance. With this much market representation arriving at disparate but equally important levels of support simultaneously, the likelihood of a turn becomes very high.

Taken alone, either of these levels could comprise a Work-Done target to the potential finished business of their respective trends, but occurring

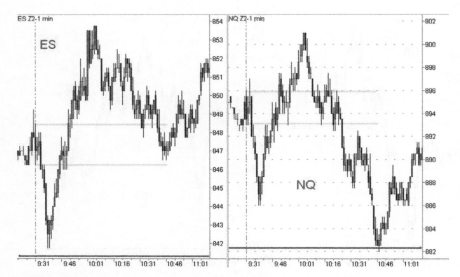

FIGURE 17.2 ES and NQ now React to Simultaneous Supports

simultaneously near the end of the 10:30 A.M. Trend Check suggests a confluence that would encourage a fresh trade entry in the opposite direction. Figure 17.2 displays the follow-up action.

The last 15 minutes of both charts in Figure 17.2 show a bounce from those respective support levels, sending price trending back upward. A new bullish swing had begun. A similar set of concepts, but with different particulars, would call an end to this new bullish trend as well, just a short time later, seen in Figure 17.3.

A Pivot Ledge left open from the NQ decline, right at the lower part of the NQ's Opening Range, obstructs the NQ bullish trend, at least for the short term. The ES has bounced off its ORB, and has been taken to new intraday highs, a level of potential exhaustion. The end of the 1st Frame is at hand as the clock reaches 11:15 A.M., and yet the market, if considered as a whole, has really accomplished little in the way of daily trend. Taken as simultaneous technical accomplishments, the trade action at this new juncture of development would suggest a fresh set of positions with a turn-and-reverse strategy from long contracts back into shorts.

With so much ORB relationship disparity between two such leading market sectors as those represented by the ES and NQ, the market as a whole on the day in question in Figures 17.1–17.3 might easily be trapped in a trading range for the day. But the intraday trader doesn't know the eventual outcome of the day's trend. In fact, he doesn't care. The economic news

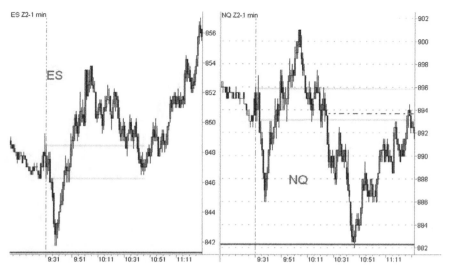

FIGURE 17.3 ES, NQ Bounce Finds Mutual Exhaustion and Resistance

that comes and goes at 10:00 A.M., or earlier economic numbers typically announced around 8:30 A.M., *pre-cash* in the morning, are totally irrelevant to his decisions. All that type of thinking relates to where the market is *supposed* to go. The Trader has forgotten where the road leads. His focus is only on where the road has taken him at this moment in time, at the right edge of his video screen. The Trader's job is not to predict but to position, and then manage the position until either it is stopped out by a signal that did not work, reaches the target of Work-Done trend business, or arrives at another set of confluent technical aspects of disparate but simultaneous task. His operation is to *swing* his trade entries from one point of confluence to the next. See the next outcome of the current example in Figure 17.4

The example used above illustrates the simplest of event concepts. It comprises disparate price supports achieved by separate index contracts simultaneously near a static Time Marker. Any combination of technical event concepts that arrive simultaneously can contribute to an Entry Model. There is a near infinite pool of possibilities from which to draw. Typically, the best Entry Models will include at least one element from each of the three categories of price level, time-of-day, and pattern formation, achieved from among two or more of the four main stock index contracts simultaneously.

Study the three charts contained side-by-side in Figure 17.5 from June 13, 2013, for their combined contribution to the potential of this next Trade Entry Model.

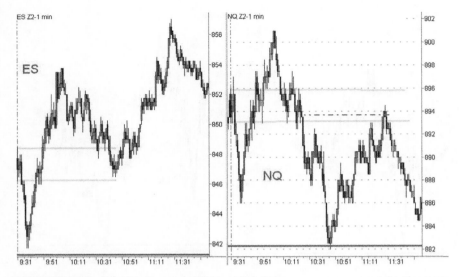

FIGURE 17.4 ES, NQ Contracts Turn at Resistance

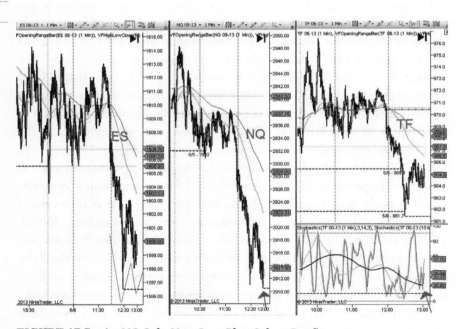

FIGURE 17.5 An NQ Solo New Low Plus Other Confluence

Consider how each contract contributed technical aspects to the totality of the Event Model. All three contracts made new lows at 12:28 P.M., just shortly after the Noon Hour. The TF contract had clipped a monthly low, marked with the dark blue dashed line that dated back to May 9. The subsequent ES retest action of its nearby low some minutes later plotted a higher low, creating a potential right shoulder for a W-Bottom reversal pattern, as suggested by the dotted red lines. Below the TF's price chart, in a Stochastic Grid window, the TF contract's pair of 10-minute momentum plots crossed up from the required indicator extreme low and was then split by a pullback of the 1-minute momentum line for the completed Stochastic Split Signal, indicating the TF retest selling would not break to a new low to follow the NQ. And the finishing piece was created by the NQ itself, which—simultaneous to the other two signals—put in a Solo New Low. This is the confluence of a completed Event Model, including pattern, time-of-day, index divergence, and momentum leadership. Note the outcome in Figure 17.6.

Now study for a moment the course of the ensuing rally in Figure 17.6 and note where the rally met the most serious resistance. In the ES and TF contracts, price had significant pullback reactions after spiking through the top of their respective upper ORB boundaries, a.k.a., the Kilroy. Then for the TF contract, note how the next surge upward was contained again at

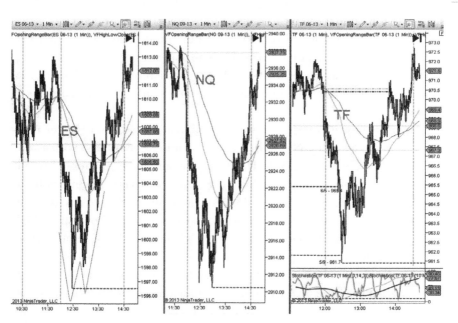

FIGURE 17.6   An Event Model Payoff

the Break-away Lap, indicated by the dotted orange and black lines. If the trader makes a practice of releasing positions into price spikes that reach such targets, he can better judge the subsequent opportunities to reenter, if any, from the comfort of a flat position on the sidelines, profits in hand. Trying to survive the price rejection of such resistance concepts should only be applied to remaining *position runners*, if any, as these support/resistance areas are capable of halting a budding trend dead in its tracks. See Chapter 18, "The Trade Plan," for position management strategies.

It's difficult as the trend is turning to know sometimes the exact 1-minute bar during which to commit. Many traders use the breakout trigger of a higher high immediately after an identified bull reversal from such a low-of-day as a form of confirmation and to ease the difficulty of pulling the trigger manually. After all, a stop-entry order executes automatically without any further assistance. But a Solo New Low by a lagging index contract can also act as the missing trigger, and provide an entry price that's much more favorable than the fill of a breakout trigger further along the budding reversal trend.

It may seem jarring to pull the trade entry trigger at the moment the NQ or YM is making a Solo High or Low, but with a little experience, that final element added to a confluence of technical signals can alleviate a great deal of the Trader's doubt as to the exact minute the trade should be entered.

It is quite common for the NQ or YM to put in these Solo New High/Low signals, but in truth it can be accomplished by any of the four contracts. Since the TF contract is the least likely to lag and the most likely to turn first in a reversal formation, it is also the least likely to appear as a Solo High/Low.

(For another example of the Solo High/Low signal as a key element to a Trade Entry Model, see the supplemental website link as per instructions in Appendix A.)

Unfortunately, it is not always possible to isolate an exact trigger minute to execute an entry. Not having a precise minute identified with a contributing concept like the Solo High/Low means the event model might take shape over some short period of time as the various elements build together into a recognizable whole. But other more exact entry triggers can arrive with a spike through a previously unchallenged overnight high or low, or the acquisition of trend resistance from a larger 60-minute time frame trend line.

Consider this next example of a Trade Entry Model in Figure 17.7. First, be aware that the day previous to the one shown, Monday, July 1, 2013, had been a Persistent Trend Day Up, not shown. The day in view, July 2, shows strong follow-through action into the Midday Frame. From that point of

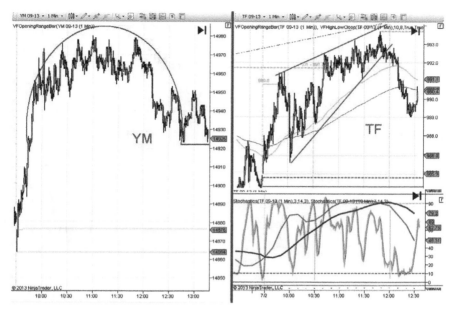

FIGURE 17.7 A Trade Entry Model Gathers Its Elements

view, part of the eventual Entry Model was in place for several hours before the other pieces began to fall in place. Study Figure 17.7.

The most significant number from the whole Pivot/Exhaustion Grid was barely visible near the top of the TF chart as a dotted red line, carried over from from a rising channel of resistance in the all-session, 60-minute chart of the TF. Spiking to that trend line at the exact Noon Hour on a day that followed a Persistent Trend Day Up, with YM divergence and momentum peaking, would have provided an exact minute for a completed Trade Entry Model.

However, price never quite reached that higher rising trend line, and turned down just before Noon. Further signals added to the Event Model, but were no clearer as trade entry triggers. The breakdown of the Rising Diagonal Wedge reversal pattern did not come with a clear Pre-Breakdown Pause Pattern, and instead was rather sloppy. The best entry prices for the signal were clearly getting away. And yet a confluence of technical events was clearly at hand.

It wasn't until a bounce by the TF pushed the 1-minute stochastic line back up into the split of the down-crossing 10-minute stochastic pair for the completed StochSplit signal did a clear trigger moment finally appear for the entry. And if the previous day's Persistent Trend Day Up was to get its usual correction, there should be a lot of room left on the downside.

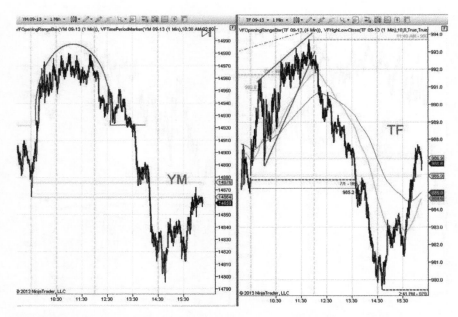

FIGURE 17.8 The Outcome: Trend Swings to the 2:30 Transition Time

Even the minimum targets provided by the YM's Cup-n-Saucer and the TF's Rising Wedge left room for a decent trade whose entry was well below the top, as can be seen in Figure 17.8.

Note that there was no way to have predicted that price would continue crashing through the respective ORBs of the YM and TF contracts. A partial position exit at that level would have certainly seemed a wise strategy on many a day. But a runner would have survived a series of trailing stop-loss levels until a reversal near the 2:30 Transition Time checked the decline, bringing prices back in each to the ORB. You can't predict. You can only position. And once in the position, you can manage a participation in the excursion, and cue off the technical elements as they appear near the right edge of the video screen. If your remaining position has survived an excursion from one Time Marker to another, you've probably acquired most of the potential opportunity.

The technical elements of Event Model don't always provide perfect clarity to the entry. It's an imperfect world. As price broke down from the Rising Wedge in Figure 17.8, it was apparent that the trend line from the 60-minute frame would not be achieved, nor would there be a further push up nearer the Noon Hour to provide another attempt at it. Instead, those subsequent breakdown signals provided the trader with invaluable information. He exchanged a near-perfect trade entry opportunity at the high for a set of confirmation values that encouraged an entry lower down. This is typical when using the static Time Markers as technical elements. The confluence often assembles itself into the whole technical picture over a narrow range of time, and often tips its hand only after the reversal has actually begun. A more precise entry trigger nearer the excursion's price extreme is always desired, but the Trader deals with what is offered, if it is offered at all.

Although the trend in this next example is from the opposite direction, there are general similarities between the Trade Entry Model in Figure 17.9 and the one depicted above in Figure 17.8. Compare them for a moment, and then consider the points that follow just for Figure 17.9.

Both contracts left a Time Marker behind them before the reversal was clearly in place. In this case, the TF did reach a critical piece of the Pivot/ Exhaustion Grid as it closed an older Open Gap after taking out an older Y-Low, unlike the action in Figure 17.8 where TF failed to quite reach the critical trend line resistance number from the 60-minute, all-session time frame. But catching the TF with buy orders at the moment of that Gap Close would have been a difficult and risky trade entry without further Entry Model elements in place.

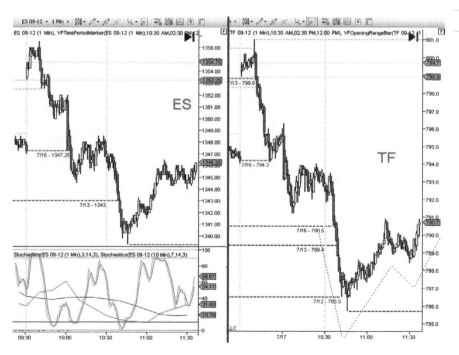

FIGURE 17.9   ES and TF Form a Trade Entry Model

It was nearly 50 minutes later and a great deal of expended patience before a narrow pullback in the ES provided the StochSplit entry, and even that would have been difficult for the Trader to catch. But consider all the confirmation that delay subsequently provided. If price broke up sharply from that level, as the change in momentum and the TF W-Bottom Reversal Pattern suggested it would, no further lows after the 10:30 A.M. Trend Check would likely have been made. And if no new lows are made after 10:30 A.M., the day more likely becomes a Test-and-Reject Day Model, not a Persistent Trend Day Down, and therefore targets a return to the ORB and perhaps higher. At some points the decision regarding trend is actually simpler than it seems otherwise. If the trend can't go further down as the clock runs out, it has to go up. See Figure 17.10.

Consider the difficulty in catching the trend at its most extreme price point. A good deal of confluence must arrive just perfectly in order for the Trader to assume such risks. But once in place, with a confluence of Work-Done finished business and Time Markers present, entry techniques that are fraught with failure if attempted too soon reward the Trader with immediate payoffs now that the Event Model is in place. These entry techniques include retests of the price extreme, especially with the StochSplit Signal for momentum, but also breakout entries in the direction of the new trend, by means of stop-entry orders placed just beyond short-term pullbacks. In

CONFLUENCE AND EXECUTION

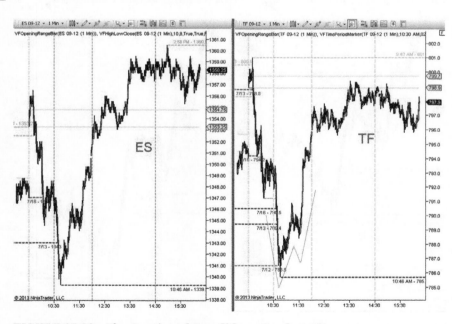

FIGURE 17.10   The Continued Payoff from Confirmation

this way, the impulse breakout itself can be captured without having had a precise minute such as a Solo New Low to trigger an entry with.

Start with the Day Model Sequence. Identify the most recent Persistent Trend Day. If this is the day after, observe whether there is further follow through in the same direction, or a correction has begun already from the ORB. If a correction has already begun, as in Figure 17.8, remember that the underlying momentum of the Persistent Trend Day will eventually come bubbling back to the surface when the correction is over. If the beginning of the correction is difficult to catch from the early ORB pattern action, then it might be just as easy to look for the price rejection area, and wait for trade signals back in the direction of the recent Persistent Trend. Although no two Event Models are ever precisely the same, the confluence of basic technical elements reviewed in the previous chapters repeats itself in unending cycles from week to week.

Consider the next example in Figure 17.11.

FIGURE 17.11 A Corrective Trend Hits Confluence

The day was July 5, 2013, and regular market trading hours had resumed after the business holiday. July 3 had been a Persistent Trend Day Up (not shown). And price gapped open sharply higher at levels achieved by the thin holiday trading hours of the electronic-only markets. The YM, NQ, and ES charts (not shown) were in perfect sync with the TF contract. All four were closing the same gap, clipping their overnight lows, and spiking into their respective 1300EMA and SMA line plots. Even the 89 and 200EMAs of all four contracts were just then crossing to the downside, another typical signal that price was due a turn, and all this right at the 10:30 A.M. Trend Check. The entire breadth of the market had reached the same support and exhaustion levels at the same time, include a clip of all four contract overnight lows, making for a very rare moment of confluence. This would be enough for this Trader to actually catch the proverbial piano and risk entering trades at the lows.

But let's assume the Trader did not, and work through the entire set of technical events that ensued. An early pennant reversal breakout, with a Time Marker reversal well behind the action, is a second and excellent place to trigger into a trade, as seen in that same Figure 17.11. Think of it in similar terms as the concept of a Pre-Breakout Pause Pattern, but back into the direction of a reversal, rather than out of a larger pattern of consolidation. It acts as a precise entry trigger, if indeed a confluence of support and exhaustion numbers have already been hit by at least two of the four main index contracts, to produce a reversal near a Time Marker.

If the breakout is sharp, a Pivot Ledge will be left in its wake, revealing a great deal of pent-up energy for the reversal trend. It's from this Pivot Ledge we acquire the Inverse 78.6% trend target. The target becomes part of the Event Model, clearing the way for a number of potential entry and reentry opportunities as the trend continues to develop. And if price is breaking away from the lows rather continuing to new price extremes, a Persistent Trend Day Down is now very unlikely. A Test-and-Reject Day is now in play, and the trading opportunities are taken accordingly. If one of the Day Models has been eliminated, the other one is now in play. If price can't proceed into the current trend, it's going to reverse into a new one.

Continue to study Figure 17.11. Reversal price action subsequently met the expected short-term resistance of the 200EMA and pulled back to the support of the pennant's apex. But the momentum has already turned up, and in conjunction with the StochSplit Signal, this pullback provides a third chance to enter in the new direction, away from the rejected lows. Now let's examine the developing trend, as seen in Figure 17.12.

FIGURE 17.12 The Test-and-Reject Event Model Progresses

In Figure 17.12, a breakout spike has taken price into a potential Noon Hour High, where partial profits could certainly be taken. But within an hour, a Midday Channel had developed, replete with a jagged high-low range. A successful breakout would suggest a Measured Move of equal distance from the low of the day to a possible target above, matching the target already in place from the Inverse 78.6% Projection Rule, as drawn on the chart from the initial Pivot Ledge. It is important to stress that the targets created from a successful breakout after a Test-and-Reject reversal are part of the Event Model itself. The targets and the Event Model should be thought of as one.

Continue studying Figure 17.2. After the Channel breakout, the Kilroy price extreme at the upper range of the ORB just around the 2:30 Transition Time was the wise trader's exit strategy. And from the relative comfort of a flat, or near-flat contract position, the Trader could more easily observe fresh reentry possibilities. The pullback to the cupping 200EMA could have inspired a low risk reentry. The EMAs had flipped, with the faster 89 now on top, supporting the change of trend. That would have been the fifth in-trend entry opportunity associated with this Trade Model, not counting the low itself at the 10:30 Trend Check.

But trading opportunities for in-trend entries were not over just yet for the Trade Entry Model of Figure 17.12. A clear, Pre-Breakout Pause Pattern appeared on the retest of the Kilroy, at the upper end of the ORB. Another buy-stop entry order could have been place just a tick above that pause pattern to trigger a position up to the pair of matching targets suggested earlier by the Midday Channel's Measured Move and the Inverse 78.6% Projection Rule. And with that final trigger beyond the ORB, those targets were both achieved just near the end of the day for a full intraday swing excursion. Work-Done.

■ Summary

Any combination of technical event minutia that arrives simultaneously can contribute to an Entry Model. Although they are by no means an exhaustive list of technical tools, those in this book were chosen for their consistency and simplicity. Typically, the best Entry Models will include at least one element from each of the three categories of price level, time-of-day, and pattern formation, achieved from among two or more of the four main stock index contracts simultaneously.

An Event Model does not always come together in a single minute. Often the Day-Model Sequence Cycle provides the first element of the Trade Entry Model many hours before the market is even open. One of the four main Time Markers is not always immediately in view as a price reversal shows up. And a recognizable entry trigger may not appear until there's a good deal of pattern development already pushing the trend away from the more ideal price opportunity. A clear breakout pattern trigger or a Solo High/Low event at the turn provides the best entry spot, if a confluent set of technical events are also in place. Sometimes it's the delayed breakout trigger itself, as from a small pennant that develops soon after the reversal has begun, that confirms the reversal, and in so doing projects the excursion to the new trend's target.

And finally, it takes a great deal of discipline to wait for a complete Trade Model to form. No Entry Model is perfect or repeats itself with perfect consistency. Therefore, both the inconsistency in the marketplace and the Trader's own inconsistency of behavior need to be managed if performance is to come anywhere near the profit opportunities contained in Technical Event Models. The management of limiting one's trade behavior to the qualifications of Trade Entry Models is the stuff of a Trade Plan, as discussed in the next chapter.

CHAPTER 18

The Trade Plan

M ost of the time and money expended on trading education is in pursuit of better technical tools. The less successful trader wants to know
the more successful trader's methods. He believes that if only he too can
learn the tricks of the better trader, he will become more profitable and be
free of the seemingly insurmountable challenge presented in mastering the
markets. And yet, the glaring reality in the world of trading education shows
a very low success rate to the transfer of skills. Furthermore, of those within
the trading community known for their success, none seem to use the same
methods. So then, some other factor must be in play.

The statistics of losers to winners in the world of trading is not encouraging. Some industry studies track the opening of commodity futures accounts
and note that nearly 90 percent of them fail to sustain enough profit to
remain open after even one year of trading. It's highly likely then that those
percentages also apply to the audience of this book. And I believe I know
why. Over some 30 years' experience as a broker, a mentor, an educator,
an analyst, a speaker, a trader, and an author I can attest to the fact that the
majority of those I've worked with simply do not trade with a plan, nor have
ever even constructed one.

When I first begin to mentor a trader, the subject comes quickly to what
he or she knows and looks at in order to follow and interpret market action.
But when I ask to see the specific document used to govern the activity of
trading, no such document exists to review.

Instead, what I have observed is that the mass of traders who approach
the markets usually trade with various forms of decision support, and may,
in fact, continue to build on their base of knowledge and understanding in
the use of trading tools as their experience grows. But they almost never

limit their trading behavior to anything other than the dollar amount left in their account before looking for a better set of tools or tricks in the hopes of improving the outcome. Seldom do I ever witness a set of rules established for the specific qualification of trade entries that would prevent the use of intuition. And instead, most of the addition of new technical tools is used quite intentionally to improve the outcome of what might be called *tape reading*. Most traders seem to believe that their role is to figure out which way the market is trying to go in real time with whatever resources of understanding and observation they can bring to bear on it at any given moment, rather than looking for a set of pre-specified technical attributes that have arrived regardless of which way the trader might be assuming the market is trying to go. This is a distinction with a difference.

When considering what is actually encompassed by the activity of trading as a whole, it must be acknowledged that the Trader really plays multiple roles. He must first be an *accountant* and manage the funds as a business. He therefore feels the pressure of responsibility and the consequence of losses. He must next be a market *analyst* and an interpreter of data, and so operates under the constant threat to his intellectual integrity the potential of being proven wrong. And lastly, he must conduct with independence the activity of *trade execution* to maximize returns and minimize losses, while the emotional influences from the other two roles continue in their attempts to guide his hand.

The problem comes when the division of this labor is left unclear, and presents itself as overlapping and conflicting impulses to drive the activity in real time. The Accountant role fears the effects of losses to the point of driving the activity irrationally toward loss recovery, no matter what the risk. The Analyst role sees the markets as an intellectual challenge and is geared toward proving he is right while denying when he's wrong. And the Trader, if left without authority in the business, is little more than the point of keyboard and mouse-click access, rather than an executor of a specific plan. He does what he's told. He knows no other.

■ Prescript

The purpose of the Trade Plan is to establish a specific and fixed set of rules for trade activity that must be adhered to during trading hours irrespective of the ever-changing nature of market conditions. Furthermore, by establishing a permanent Trade Plan, the activities of the total business are set to distinguish and separate the individual roles. Each is accorded a place and time for their specific contributions. The Accountant and the Analyst are accorded time for the contribution of their roles outside—but never during—the time in which trading is actually taking place. With their contributions now committed to the Plan, the singular role of the Trader is raised to that of Executor of the Business. By virtue of this authority, the Trader enters only those trades—but all of those trades, as evidenced by the pre-market work of the Analyst—which match a set of specified criteria for Technical Trade Entry Models. Furthermore, to serve the responsibilities without serving the real-time emotions of the Accountant, the Trader will be further governed by the Accountant's pre-sets; that of trade frequency limits, risk-to-profit ratios, maximum loss triggers, and profit goal measurements of all current activity according to such guidelines as documented in the Plan.

The Plan is to be established with great care and consideration, for it must be executed with commitment and consistency once in place. The Plan is never changed on the fly during a trading day. Potential Entry Models uncovered by the Analyst must meet the criteria of a solid positive percentage in outcome before agreed upon for inclusion in the Plan by the Accountant and the Trader. Furthermore, once included, Trade Entry Models are not removed from the Plan on any initial failure. Likewise, once included in the Trade Plan, the Trader executes trade positions for any Entry Model that appears, as long as the technical filters included in that model do not invalidate its execution, regardless of which way any of the three identity roles of the business may believe the market is supposed to go, or which way any of them assess the market is trying to go.

In other words, the Trader operates as a plan of action a set of rules that compel him to make—and prevent him from taking—action as per the rules as they are met or qualified. Therefore, a Trade Plan actually demands the Trader take trades he might not agree with emotionally at that moment, and prevents him from taking trades based simply on which way it appears the market is trying to go. There are no gut feelings about the market. There is no tape reading. Intuition is not permitted as an element of decision support, and is not a filter to a qualified Trade Entry Model.

The Analyst does not execute trades, nor is he allowed to test his prowess against market conditions in real time in order to prove how right he can be. The Accountant is never allowed to try to recoup the desperation of his losses, no matter how unsettling the emotions that drive him to do so before the market closes, upon a day's summation. His job is to keep the books on profits and losses, see that capital commitments have strict requirements, and establish a consequence to performance. For the Trader, there is only recognition and commitment. His character is called upon to impose discipline to the Plan. The Trader is the rule of law. The Accountant and the Analyst were the authors. If they want the Trader to operate under modifications to the Plan, the terms must be renegotiated outside of market hours.

An itemized performance summary will be kept each day, with each trade identified in the summary according to an associated acronym or abbreviation for the preapproved Entry Model employed. A running performance statement is kept of all trades for comparison against daily, weekly, and monthly profit goals. A trade cessation trigger is tripped as a kind of action stop-loss by any succession of losing trades. It is thus that remaining capital can be preserved and problems identified quickly. A real-time trade platform simulator is used as a fallback strategy to regroup and practice after such action triggers are tripped. Continued feedback regarding Plan performance will induce changes to the Plan before further trading resumes. And a constant critique of the Plan's execution will be conducted in a Daily Journal, to be sent to and witnessed by anyone outside of the Trader's own realm by whom his business might be held accountable.

And yes, let's hope that sounded enough like a legal document to impose the degree of sincerity on the task that a Trade Plan is meant to instill.

■ Blueprint

The following is a generic outline for a Trade Plan. The most important aspect of the Trade Plan is that it must be adhered to. Therefore, the specifics really cannot be copied from someone else. In order for the Trader to truly commit to the Plan, he must believe that its guidelines are practical, wise, and have a strong historical success record. Each must establish his own. And the best way to *own* a set of guidelines is to author them first, and then make adjustments begrudgingly as needed, but only after some due consideration outside of market hours. The Plan is never changed on the fly.

Where appropriate to the blueprint following, I have added my preferences. Clearly, this outline is geared toward using the technical concepts exposed in this book. If the Trader prefers others, substitute those. Naturally, my own Plan includes some concepts not taught in this book, especially the signals from the Serial Sequent Wave Method, requiring a software algorithm. Even if none of the concepts in this book have sparked enough interest for the reader to incorporate them, it is sincerely hoped that the message about needing a Trade Plan will inspire the reader to create one using specific models of his own design or research.

Trade Model Criteria
Tier1 Entry Model Specs
    Test-and-Reject Day Model Sequence stipulation
    Time Marker inclusive
    Classic Chart Pattern in a second contract
    Key support/resistance/exhaustion in two of four contracts
    Stochastic Momentum Signal
    Clear entry trigger present
Tier2 Entry Model Specs
    Test-and-Reject Day Model Stipulation
    2nd Trend Test-and-Reject Stipulation
    ORB or other support/resistance level identified
    Stop-n-Reverse trigger entry identified
Tier3 Entry Model Specs
    Day Model Sequence acknowledgment
    Time Marker inclusive
    Key support/resistance/exhaustion in two of four contracts
    No clear entry trigger available
Tier4 Entry Model Specs
    Day Model Sequence acknowledgment
    Opening Range proximity
    Selected ORB Breakout Pattern requirement
Tier5 Entry Model Specs
    Day Model Sequence acknowledgment
    1st or Midday Frame trading range established
    Retest congestion pattern established
    Pre-Breakout Pause Pattern trigger apparent
Tier6 Entry Model Specs
    Day Model identity established
    Noon Hour or 2:30 Time Marker dependent
    Key support/resistance/exhaustion in two of four contracts
    Divergence in two of four contracts
    Clear entry trigger present

Mechanical Behavior Governors

Trade frequency limitations
   Total trades per frame
   Total trades per day
   Total losing trades in a row
   Total number of losing days in a row
   Total number of losing weeks in a row
   Consequences
$$ loss limits
   Total risked for a full position
   Total loss limit for the frame
   Total loss limit for a single day
   Total loss limit for a single week
   Consequences
Profit goals
   Daily
   Weekly
   Monthly
   Consequences

Position Management Strategies and Methods

Tiers 1 and 4: 3-unit position requirement
   All in, simultaneous entries
   Partial out initial exit, adjust stops
   Partial out 2nd-exit mechanical target
   Last unit runner, stop trails only after all retests
Tiers 2, 3, and 5: 2-unit position
   Without clear trigger, stagger the entries
   With clear trigger, simultaneous entries
   Quick partial out of 1st unit, 2nd unit to net b/e stop
All positions managed with OCO orders
   OCO auto-management via trade software platforms (e.g.,
      ChartTrader and SuperDom from NinjaTrader.com, or viable
      competitors)

Daily Journaling

- Should begin with a simplified version of your trade summary for the day.

- Must be done after each day's trading.

- Should be done in a public way that can be read by someone to whom you owe some responsibility or explanation regarding your commitment to trading.

- Should be positive in nature overall, with a tone of belief in one's abilities to eventually meet the challenges at hand.

- Should be brutally honest about trading errors, mental blocks, trepidations regarding trade entries, trend prejudices, affectations from news or economic events, and so forth.

- Should contain comments both about the Plan itself and your adherence or failure of adherence to the Plan. Include any insights for self-improvements, and any open-ended questions that yet need answers on any trading subject or any aspect of the mental game of trading as a business.

- Can include screen captures of Technical Event Models as occurred in that day's trading to assist in Trade Plan improvement, modification, recognition practice, and so forth.

■ My Blueprint Notes

The following text should be taken as my personal conclusions regarding a Trade Plan. These might be used as very general suggestions or insights into the process of creating and being guided by a Trade Plan. But as previously stated, a Trade Plan must be individualized. The very process of creating it gives it an added meaning to the Trader. It should never be wholly borrowed or duplicated from another trader. If the Trader cannot commit to his Entry Models, especially when his emotions tell him to ignore it, the whole purpose of having a plan begins to break down. Once broken, a Trade Plan can quickly become worthless. Instead, the Trader should minutely examine any juncture where it was ignored in order to expose the conflicting emotions and/or mental blocks that prevented the Plan from being followed. This examination might lead to modifying the Plan, but even better, if the Plan is truly valid, such Plan violations and their corresponding critique can facilitate the very difficult process of behavior modification required of the Trader to succeed.

My Trade Model Criteria
I take screen captures for a visual description of every Entry Model in my Plan. I keep a library of these Entry Models in subdirectories by acronym.

See Appendix E on how to automate this process to run unnoticed in the background every day.

I divide Trade Entry Models into a classification system that helps accentuate risk and opportunity. I define the best opportunities under Tiers 1 and 5. Tier 1 has the most complete confluence of Entry Model elements. Tier 5 is associated with Pre-Breakout Pause Patterns, and when further associated with pattern failure, can produce some of the more extended trends within the intraday frame. Tiers 2, 3, 4, and 6 have fewer complete Event Model characteristics, but cover a fairly large majority of trade opportunities from day to day.

I find that some of the best information available to improve trading is found within one's own trade history. By dividing Event Models into classes or types, it is easier to review and identify what trade types are working and which are producing the most losses.

My Mechanical Behavior Governors

I try to limit my total trades per day to 10. My better days are usually accomplished when I only take five trades or less. The degree to which I violate this limitation is usually the degree to which I am having a bad day.

I don't allow myself more than three losing trades in a row. I do not add net break-even trades to this loss limitation count. A losing trade is a full stop-out of my position, not a stop-out at break-even or net break-even. Net break-even occurs when part of the position was exited at a profit, but the remainder was stopped out at a loss about equal to the partial profit.

The consequences I imposed on my trading after three losing trades in a row is a sentence on the trade simulator. Once on the simulator, I can only take trades from my Entry Models, just as in real trading. If I profit on two of three trades or three of five trades in a row, I am allowed to return to trading real money that same day, if there's any time left in that day. If not, I must quit for the day. I am allowed to trade real money on the following day.

At no time do I ever allow myself to trade the simulator on intuition or by means of tape reading. Introducing these habits into trading even during simulation is like a disease, difficult to cure.

If I lose two days in a row, I must begin the next day on the trade simulator, always limiting my trades to those in my Trade Plan. Again, after two of three winning trades I am allowed to trade with real money again that day, and am subject again to the same set of loss limitation rules.

If I have a net losing week, I must begin the next week on the simulator, and again earn the right to trade with real money. These rules are designed to established consistency. For a new trader, such rules can facilitate pulling the plug on the whole operation or set of Trade Models before the entire commitment of capital has been lost.

Two net losing weeks of intraday trading in a row is a trigger to review the entire operation. Examine the trade journal closely. Did all the Entry Models fail to show the anticipated outcomes? Did I suffer the consequences of having entered before the model was fully in place? Were the profits from successful models insufficient to cover the losses from those trades that were unsuccessful? What were the precise causes of my unprofitable trades? Did I manage the trades too poorly, and fail to capture a sufficient portion of their maximum excursions? Did every trade I list in the trade summary have an acronym identifying it to one my Entry Models? If not, why not? Am I slipping out of my Entry Models to take trades based on either intuition, or a desire to recover from a previous losing trade? Am I failing to enter each trade in my journal in the first place? Am I failing the Plan, or is the Plan failing me?

The consequence to meeting a daily profit goal is to stop trading for the day. This sounds like a negative consequence, but from my experience, increasing the frequency of trades usually adjusts the profit to loss ratio downward. There is no consequence to meeting a weekly profit goal before the fifth day of trading that week. The consequence of meeting a monthly profit goal before the last day's trading in the month is a requirement to take a day away from the markets. The consequence of meeting a year's worth of monthly profit goals is to up the number of contracts used for a Tier 1 Trade Event Model. This may seem like a very tame addition to risk management, but experience has taught me that the worst periods of losses to profits have always come following an increase in the number of contracts used per trade. This, I believe, is an indication that certain risk thresholds can have a cumulative, geometric increase in psychological pressures over the mere arithmetic increase that an additional risk would otherwise imply.

If I am failing the Plan in any way, I post the exact nature of those failures each day in the Journal, whenever it occurs, no matter how often it occurs. I publish the Journal on line, and it's linked to a menu button on the website for valhallafutures.com, labeled Daily Blog. The Journal can also be accessed directly at valhallafutures.blogspot.com. The Daily Journal also includes a summary of my trade results for that day.

There should be a tone and temperament to the Daily Journal. On the one hand, an upbeat mood with a positive expectancy should permeate the voice you use to journal your thoughts. On the other hand, a brutal honesty should expose your failings, always accompanied by constructive self-criticism as to how to proceed and improve.

I'm told I tend to lean a little hard on the brutal honesty side of self-criticism, and am rather deficient in the application of the cheerleading mode. I just can't believe how stupid I can be at times, and often feel the need to carry over into real time the awareness of those mistakes I make repeatedly in a more conspicuous manner.

Behavior is a very difficult thing to change. And some of the best Trade Entry Models in my repertoire go unexecuted due to trepidations regarding trend prejudice. Perhaps I was destined just to teach, as so many of my students become far better traders than myself.

My Position Management Strategies and Methods

A clear entry trigger can make all the difference to an Entry Model. Some conditions reveal a breakout pattern, some reveal a fairly fine-tuned pullback level, but some only provide an entry zone, where several contracts have reached good support/resistance/exhaustion levels simultaneously. Putting your position all-in immediately doesn't allow for the market to find its own base, which may be slightly above or below the precise numbers initially associated with those identified price levels. When in such a zone of entry, taking 2nd-unit positions at a better price can dramatically improve the possibilities of a successful trade. Life is imperfect, and on many days, I get stopped out of a developing Event Model only to reenter it if the signals are still in place.

It is hard to imagine trading index futures in the fast-paced environment of intraday trend action without pre-set OCO order strategies. OCO stands for "one cancels the other." A pre-set OCO strategy will automatically place both a default stop-loss order and a target exit order for every open contract filled at execution. Most of my target and stop-loss adjustments are actually done by hand thereafter, as I find auto-trailing stop-loss orders to move without regard to important developments in the unfolding market structure of real-time action. But placing those initial stop-loss and target orders manually, the old fashioned way, without an initial automatic OCO bracket, is a recipe for disaster in the world of derivatives. I notice that some beginner traders believe the added expense to lease trade management software (such as that offered from NinjaTrader.com), is an added expense they cannot afford. This assessment simply fails to acknowledge the additional losses that will occur without it, quickly surpassing the cost of the monthly lease rates many times over. As they say in ads, regarding a good trade management software platform, don't leave home without it.

One of the most difficult things to know in trading is when to exit. Some traders simply acknowledge that a 3-point swing in the TF contract is a fairly typical move, and therefore a mechanical exit of any remaining contracts at this profit level is a better overall bet than the risks associated with establishing a runner. Such a move might be compared to a 4-point move in the ES, a 10-point move in the NQ and 45-point in the YM.

Other traders seem to expend the extra patience required to capture the larger excursions of intraday swings between the day's key Time Frame Transitions, even if they don't even consider the existence of such Time Markers while they trade. I've had the opportunity to witness both styles of exiting from exemplary traders, and those with the greater patience and established runner positions tend to do better. But the added risk for that 2nd or 3rd unit at the initial entry levels can wipe out the beginner trader rather quickly if his Trade Entry Models are not well defined and consistently well timed.

Start small. Start on the trade simulator. Never, ever use the simulator to take trades other than those of the Entry Models within your Trade Plan. After six months of working with a trade simulator developing your Trade Plan and fine-tuning the Entry Models within it, you'll be ready to assess your results. Be brutally honest. If any of your simulator profits came from trades you took from tape reading or intuition, be mindful of this one important thing: Results from simulated trades based on intuition and tape reading cannot be duplicated in real time with real money. Everything changes. The infamous observation about life from Heraclitus holds especially true for trading, "Your character is your fate."

My Daily Journal

I just can't stress how important the Daily Journal will be to your own self-improvement. The fact that journaling is the thing done least by the majority of traders who wonder why they have been excluded from the thin minority who succeed in trading for a living should be at least a hint as to what you might be missing by not acquiring the habit. I simply cannot imagine any trader accomplishing even a modicum of the behavior change required of self-improvement without keeping a daily trade journal. I post mine from the valhallafutures.com website, through the link named Daily Blog, but you can also access it directly at http://valhallafutures.blogspot.com.

■ Summary

A Trade Plan is not just more important than the Trade Entry Models you use in the operations of trading. It is a means to the very existence and evolution of that Trade Entry Model list in the first place. There is a huge learning and experience curve to the business of trading. It's hard enough even to know where to begin. For the very beginner, a Trade Plan might be a list including technical subjects that are yet to be learned, software to be acquired, trading platforms to be mastered, capital to be accumulated, methods to be discovered, and other relevant topics. Eventually, as those items are ticked off the experience and acquisition list, real strategies emerge to actually enter trades, and a Plan is in the formation. Add into it precise Entry Model identification and the feedback loop of a Daily Journal, and a beginner is well on his way. Unless of course he or she is like the 90 percent of traders who simply open brokerage accounts, join some chat room or other, learn to read the signals from a technical indicator or two, and throw seed capital at the intellectual and egocentric pursuit of trying to intuit in real time which way the market is trying to go.

Don't throw your seed capital at trying to intuit in real time which way the market is trying to go. Create a Trade Plan, even if in its earliest stages it is more a to-do list than a method of taking trades. Then, when a page or two of that has been written, open a public document, preferably on the Internet in some form of social media, and make the first entry of your future Daily Journal. It might read something like this: *Today I started a plan for the business of trading stock index futures. I already have this, that, and the other. What I need to learn is that, the other, and this. The learning curve looks pretty steep. I hear a lot of people lose money doing this. But I've decided to create a well-defined strategy to take advantage of some of the unique and regular profit opportunities it offers. Stay tuned. Tomorrow, I'll take another step forward. I'm pretty excited about the whole thing. I'll let you know how far I get each day right here. I know I'm going to need a lot of help. Comments welcomed.*

Companion Website

Wiley Trading has supplied a companion website to selected authors in its library. This provides space for more examples of the concepts presented in this book, and colorized chart versions of selected grayscale figures that appear throughout the text, to better serve those readers who have purchased the print or digital editions. The website for *Pivots, Patterns, and Intraday Swing Trades* can be found at www.wiley.com/go/scheier. Then enter the PIN code found at the back of this book. E-book readers will also find additional instructions for requesting a PIN code.

Once there, you'll find a table of contents that matches the one in this book. Where pertinent, a chapter will have two tabs, one for the colorized chart versions of grayscale figure examples already in the book, and a second tab for additional figure examples to supplement the author's concepts.

It is the intention of the author to update this site periodically with more examples of the concepts in this book, as they become available. Check the companion website occasionally for continued education.

Color Legend

M any elements of the Pivot/Exhaustion Grid depicted in earlier chapters project specific price levels of support, resistance, or exhaustion far into the future, beyond the right edge of the video screen. As time proceeds, price may move away from the source of these price levels for an extended period of time before returning. In order to identify the source when such levels reappear on the Trader's screen, a color code is used to assist in the identification, as well as a label depicting the exact number and the date it was incurred. A monthly low obviously has greater significance than does a daily.

Seeing unfamiliar lines reappearing on the screen days or weeks later can be confusing. The particular colors chosen are only important insofar as they serve mnemonic memory triggers. Mine are pretty obvious, but your own may be preferred; the more obvious, the better. Here are mine:

- Lines colored *cyan are for Highs, like the sky*, and those depicting *Lows are dark blue, like the sea*. Yesterday's High and Low from day-only data are plotted in a heavy dash style. Overnight High/Lows are not as critical as daily High/Lows from yesterday, so they plot with thin solid lines, but are more important than intraday High/Lows, which only plot with thin, dotted lines. All these lines are set to *terminate-if-touched*, as their usefulness as indicators ends when broken.

- Resistance lines from the Floor Trader's Pivots grid are *lighter green, like the upper, new foliage of growing trees*, and are complimented by *dark green in the lower shadows*, with the Daily Pivot in *dark brown, like solid earth*. These too are terminate-if-touched.

- The 89EMA is *faster and lighter green* than the *older and slower* 200EMA, in *dark green*.

- The *brown* of the 1300EMA is a bit *lighter and faster* than its *older and slower dark brown* companion, the 1300SMA.

- *A stop sign ends traffic*, so *red* is used to plot the day's Closing price through the following day, terminate-if-touched. A heavy dashed line of the Y-Close is used to match the line style of the Y-High and Y-Low, also set to terminate-if-touched.

- A Break-away Lap is less important than a true Gap, so the color is orange for the Lap, red for a true daily Gap. A dash-dot-dot style for the Lap is less obtrusive than the heavy red dash of the true Gap.

- The Pivot Ledge of a Break-away Pivot can be *death to a trend* in the short term, and therefore is *black*. The plot style is the same as the Break-away Gap.

- *The day begins with sunshine*, so *yellow* is the color for the 9:30 A.M. day-only session marker, as well as the Opening Range Bar bracket plots.

- A thin red solid line depicts intraday trend lines, and a heavier red dash-dot-dot line depicts a trend line carried in from the 60-minute all-session data chart.

Once the sense of this is apparent, you'll never forget it, and can identify any line plot that reappears on the charts from any former historical period. (If you are viewing this text and the accompanying graph in Figure B.1 in

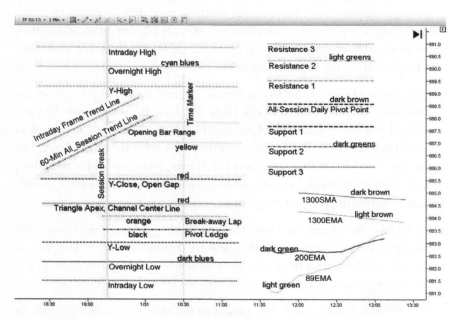

FIGURE B.1   Mnemonic Device Color Legend

e-book format, then the colorized chart is apparent. If not, you can also view the colorized version of Figure B.1 on the Wiley companion website for this book, with access instructions in Appendix A.)

The better software chart packages available today, such as the software from Ninjatrader.com, offer the ability to program such indicators to plot, label, and terminate-if-touched automatically, assuming you have the skills and the time to do the programming. Appendix D contains information about the package of indicators from ValhallaFutures that includes the Pivot/Exhaustion Grid with those features already programmed.

Serial Sequent Wave Method

There is a huge body of historical evidence, the author believes, that suggests chaos wave patterns do, in fact, repeat themselves according to some internal development structure. R. N. Elliott uncovered a method to label waves in the early part of the twentieth century, which has become an analysis practice by educators and vendors for decades, and is generally now referred to as Elliott Wave. Price history labeled by the rules of Elliott Wave seems to show good replication and some predictive qualities when comparing historical data to that of the current market charts.

One of the problems in using this method in real time is the alternative wave count subject to interpretations at any potential turning point. A trend can seem to extend indefinitely, but the limit to the count of a section of impulse trend is fixed at the maximum fulfillment count of 5. When the trend proceeds to yet another wave, the current 5 must then be carried to the new price extreme, and the previous wave must be given a new count attached to a lower subdegree of wave strength, also with the maximum 5 limitation.

At some point, there are enough subdivisions of lower degree to fulfill the needs of the highest degree, and the trend finally comes to an end. That may be just fine for the author of a newsletter who can post his analysis in arrears of the event and sort out the subdegree labels to make the formula work out perfectly. But for the Trader who must commit funds at the right edge of his video screen, these false end-of-trend signals can be quite costly.

And that only illuminates part of the problem with Elliott Wave labeling rules. All waves must be successfully identified as either *impulsive* to move in sync with the prevailing trend, or *corrective* and running counter to the prevailing trend. Corrective waves tend to overlap, and are labeled with the letters A, B, and C, while impulsive waves do not overlap and are labeled 1 through 5 only. But when corrective, overlapping waves begin to move in sync with the prevailing trend, and succeed in making new price extremes to the impulsive trend instead, a mislabeling of the wave count occurs, indicating suddenly to the Trader, who has followed the initial wave labeling rules with a real trade position, that he's actually entered in the wrong direction. Oops.

The Serial Sequent Wave Method™, uncovered by the author, makes no differentiation between impulsive and corrective wave labeling. Nor is there a 5-wave limit to a trend's excursion before being forced to relabel previous waves into subdegrees as the trend continues with fresh wave extension. An understanding of the purpose for wave labeling assumes that purpose is to identify when a section of chaos has come to an end, and when it will correct back in the opposite direction. These sections of chaos, called fractals, usually do not represent any classic chart pattern identification, but they do, however, reveal certain mathematical equations in the unfolding process. Once understood, this algorithm can be applied to any wave progress as it unfolds at the right edge of the video screen, and signal when another such section of wave fractals has come to an end.

Furthermore, the signal rules used by the algorithm's chaos analysis self-adjust according to the wave history that developed the current trend. It looks back to the *mood* that previous advances and pullbacks exposed, and carries that into the rules of the present wave label calculation. With Serial Sequent, there is no attempt to force-fit the trend into the 5-wave trend limit stipulation. Too much of the time, it simply doesn't fit. A trend has *character*, and may want to end on the 4th, 5th, or 6th extension of the chaos fractal. It may not want to end until the 11th. The Serial Sequent algorithm doesn't care. It lets the trend reveal itself according to its own internal structure requirements, not those imposed upon it from the outside.

The results are startling. Whether unraveling the internal message to overlapping waves, or those that extend without overlap in impulsive fashion, the algorithm of fractal sequent reveals that wave structure repeats an internal formula in development regardless of direction, consolidation, or trend extension considerations. It turns out that the whole impulsive-versus-corrective wave identification is an artificial consideration to the analysis, and that in reality, the underlying market is using the same formula in fractal development regardless. Think of a kind of flexible erector set that retains its structural integrity regardless of whether compressed into a channel or unfolded into one long, extended arm.

The wave labeling methods to Serial Sequent are new to wave analysis since Elliott first employed his observations. And superimposed over the Serial Sequent wave labels is a set of rules by which the Trader then incorporates these wave signals into Trade Event Models. Although this author makes the claim that Serial Sequent is the most exacting market technical minutia ever uncovered to identify trend reversal and breakout levels, it still is only part of the consideration for committing real funds to the business of derivatives trading. For a true Technical Event Model to be used as a Trade Entry Model, other technical minutia must arrive in confluence of price and time with the Serial Sequent Wave signal. It's output must be included in *Old School* trade methodology. But in and of itself, Serial Sequent is of the *New School* and requires a software algorithm.

A complete training course that incorporates the Serial Sequent Wave Method with the other key elements of identifying Trade Entry Models is available through ValhallaFutures.com. The course includes the proprietary software that utilizes the wave algorithm, and includes a number of other software indicator enhancements that automate the process of detecting and labeling the other concepts in the course. A breakdown of this package can be viewed in Appendix D.

ValhallaFutures Indicator Package and Intraday Index Futures Trading Course

The indicators and line plots used for the analysis behind the concepts of this book can, in fact, be drawn each day by hand. When the efforts required are multiplied over the four index contracts used to derive the totality of signal concepts, the task becomes a bit overbearing. Many readers may be skilled enough to program their own indicators to automate the detection, labeling, and terminate-if-touched features these indicators require. And since many traders will intend to continue using software charting packages other than that offered by NinjaTrader.com, programming skills in other languages might be required to duplicate these indicators for such automation.

The wave labels of the Serial Sequent Wave Method cannot be accomplished by hand. The formula for wave identification is based on an algorithm and remains the intellectual property of the author. The labeling indicator is included in the package, but the software code modular is locked and protected. A license and nondisclosure form must be signed with each purchase.

The list of indicators currently included in the package appears here, as taken from the installation file.

What's Included

VFIndicators_3.3.zip

VFLinkHLIn / VFLinkHLOut

This indicator automatically lifts the Globex overnight High/Low from all-session data and plots it in the day-only session charts.

VFBreak-AwayLap

This indicator comes with preference alternatives and adjustments to the Terminate-if-Touched feature, such as Show Date Label, Show Price Label, and Show Direction Arrow.

VFHighLowClose

This indicator, like all the line plot indicators in the package, includes preference alternatives to color and plot style, and comes with Terminate-if-Touched as a preference default.

VFTimePeriodMarker

Preference alternatives to color and plot style are variable.

VFOpeningRangeBar

Brackets the range for the day, terminates end-of-day, lines set to plot underneath the price bars, so as to be unobtrusive.

VFSerialSequent

Preference alternatives for label colors, spacing, fonts and look-back periods. Templates: TTI (True Trend Momentum Indicator), Stochastic Grid Momentum Indiator, Tick Bars

Compatibility

The indicators included in the package are compatible only with NinjaCharts from NinjaTrader.com, and MS Windows O/S.

ValhallaFutures Trading Course

The course includes 10, 1.5-hour lessons conducted in small groups via Internet webinars. Three of those 10 lessons specifically focus on the Serial Sequent Wave Method using software included in the course.

You may repeat the course whenever it rotates back around to Lesson I.
Continuous one-on-one mentoring is provided as needed.
Attendance in the ValhallaFutures, real-time market chat room is free.
Software package and the course are one and inseparable.
Pricing is available at ValhallaFutures.com.

Screen Capturing an Event Library

I f you are a Trader, you are a student. The condition is perpetual. The best place for your education will always be from these two sources, in the order of their appearance: the market itself, and then your trading decisions regarding it. Each day I record the market action in snapshots. I use a free downloadable software tool for this called 20/20, from By Light Technologies. You'll have to do an Internet search for it by company name in order to find a safe download link. Freeware links are frequently hijacked by malicious malware and adware sites.

The 20/20 tool is a screen-capture and image-editor device, and can run in the background with timed captures. More sophisticated screen-capture software exists, such as Snagit from TechSmith. But the auto-capture feature in Snagit disconnects if you make a manual capture that interrupts its auto-schedule.

My main desktop window contains at least three of the main stock index futures contracts in equally shared vertical panes, somewhat like what is shown in Figure 5.1 of Chapter 5. In this way, it is easy to view the disparities and confluence of technical signals simultaneously. Since the screen capture is set to about once in four minutes, the chances of capturing the markets during one of its key reversal or breakout moments during the day are very high. At the end of the day, you can flip through the subdirectory where these snapshots have been auto-stored and study those times for the possible signals they reveal. While a possible Trade Event Model is forming, I'll often drag the key relevant Stochastic Grid, TRIN, Advance-Decline,

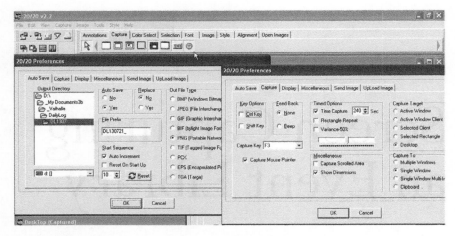

FIGURE E.1   20/20 Auto-Screen Capture Preferences

60-minute all-session chart, or other indicator window into view in order to add a manually executed screen capture to those being taken by the timed auto-capture feature.

This whole process of building a library trains your eye and mind for a more complex type of pattern recognition. Furthermore, I can then copy a particular screen capture from the subdirectory in which it was first stored into a classification subdirectory of Technical Event Model types.

This is the Analyst's best opportunity to apply his skills. Once he sees something a few hundred or even a few thousand times, it becomes familiar enough to warrant a name label. Any confluent concept that repeats itself at market turns or breakouts with frequency earns its own acronym name label and corresponding subdirectory in the concept library. Only then would such an Event Model be considered for the Trade Plan.

To set up your copy of 20/20, you can use the preferences from the dialogue boxes in Figure E.1. The mouse arrow seen pointing to the small clock face icon is the on-off switch to begin the auto-capture, auto-file naming process.

Randolph Newman

I would have never found my way into the world of derivatives trading had it not been for Randolph Newman. I was working at Maison Blanche in New Orleans, a department store run by his cousin Isadore Newman II, when Randy called during my lunch hour one day while I was out on the floor. "You've really disappointed me, son." I knew it was Randy immediately. He didn't need to say hello. I laughed. I had promised to come see him at the brokerage office where he worked, but never seemed to have found the time.

"Sorry, Randy . . . but I've just been so busy."

"Sure you have. But what are you doing right now?" he asked. He was so direct; never any small talk.

"Okay," I laughed some more. "I'll come over now during my lunch hour." And I did. It felt good to humor him. I enjoyed listening to his stories. I just figured he didn't have anyone interested in listening to them anymore.

I remember a ticker tape and a bullpen where he and a couple other futures traders were cordoned off from the rest of the office of stock brokers. He literally had a phone in each ear. It was noisy. Small colored pieces of paper were being shuffled back and forth quickly from a cashier's cage where they wired orders directly to the trading floor. I watched quietly for a few minutes. He had barely given me a nod. Breaking away from one of his phones, he handed me a small yellow note with some teletype-machine print and some additional squiggles in ink by hand. "Here," he said. "Hold onto this for me." And then went back to his phones and quote machines.

In about 15 minutes he handed me another piece of paper, apparently a match to the one I already had, but in pink. "Okay," he said. Do you have any idea what you've got there?"

"No, Randy. I don't have a clue." Apparently I'd been holding a couple hundred-weight cattle contracts.

"Now, how long have you been sitting here?" he asked.

"Huh . . ." I didn't even finish my answer.

"Right," he responded. "I just made $250.00. I heard they offered you a buyer's position over at the department store. And how much a week are they going to pay you for that now?"

That was in 1979. I think my pay at the department store was going to be raised to about $350.00 per week. Randy opened my eyes. Needless to say, I immediately switched careers.

Randolph Isadore Newman, grandson of Isadore Newman I, was from a family of financiers and traders. (See Figure F.1.) His grandfather had come to this country through the Port of New Orleans around 1851, through the same port as had my own great-great-grandfather Jacob Kremer, just one year earlier. But unlike my own immigrant ancestor, Isadore never left Louisiana. And unlike my ancestor Jacob, Isadore came penniless. Jacob at least brought a brass pot with him in which to cook his first meals for his wife and two children. We still have it.

Within a relatively short period of time, Isadore Newman had become an important money broker within the region, at one time helping to float the

FIGURE F.1 **Randolph Isadore Newman**

city of New Orleans after the post–Civil War panic of 1873. He started a cotton brokerage, founded the New Orleans Stock Exchange, and financed the Maison Blanche Department Store, the eventual flagship of City Stores Company.

Randolph, just one of Isadore's many grandchildren, was born in August 1901. He graduated from Harvard College, and later acted as Secretary-Treasurer for the Harvard Club of Louisiana. In its heyday, Randy was a floor trader at the New Orleans Cotton Exchange (NOCE). While cotton was still king, the NOCE was the world's premier go-to source for spot cotton. Later, Randy worked for a number of commodity futures brokerage firms, including Bache & Co., where I joined him, which would eventually become Prudential-Bache. Few realize the important role New Orleans and its port played in the world of commodity and equity finance. New Orleans–based Fenner & Beane was one of the largest brokerage firms in the country, and at the time of its merger, second only to Merrill Lynch. In 1941 the two firms merged to become Merrill Lynch, Pierce, Fenner & Beane.

We lost Randolph Newman in March 1982. I had only known him a few short years. His health had been declining, and he could barely make it across the street with his cane before the traffic lights would change, on the few occasions he would venture out to lunch. He taught me so much about the markets, and left me with a small treasury of market wisdom, witticism and euphemism. It took me years to understand it all. I know he'd be fascinated by all technical market concepts I picked up or uncovered along my way. I hope he'd be proud of me. He inspired me to discovery. I still miss him much.

Fibonacci versus Pivot/Exhaustion Grid

While I was writing this book, I got an e-mail solicitation for a webinar on Fibonacci trading techniques from a protégé of Robert Miner. I had studied his work and used his software many years earlier, but found the results disappointing for intraday trading of the stock index futures in the lower time frames. As discussed in Chapter 3, I still use a Fibonacci targeting rule as part of a Trade Entry Model. Out of curiosity, I attended the webinar. As a Trader, I'm a perpetual student. Always keep an open mind.

Already familiar with the techniques employed, I was reminded instead what gymnastics are engaged in order to establish an authority and credibility on market science. But isn't it perhaps already in the charts for us to understand, if only we open ourselves up to more simple observations?

The stock chart of DTV in daily bars was used for the webinar I attended, and a copy of it in Figure G.1 displays a cluster of the three targeting techniques employed. (Study Figure G.1 here, or visit the Wiley companion website for a colorized version of the Figures in Appendix G.)

The pink dashed lines plot a retracement sell-off of 61.8 percent from the high of 66 as measured from the low of 53.62. The blue dashed lines represent the 1.272 percent extension of that same sell-off, past the first leg down to the end of the second leg of selling that finished in the final days of June. And finally, the green dashed lines measure a 100 percent replay

FIGURE G.1 Fibonacci Cluster of Three Methods

distance of that same sell-off. All three cluster in approximately the same place, around $58 per share. The trend is up, so this cluster is used as a buy signal. The actual entry is delayed for confirmation and is placed at the top of a price bar that met the cluster. This delay in entry was used as confirmation to the trend, but cost nearly three points for the assurance.

Okay, fine. But the presenter really lost me when, a bit later after another example, it was stated that this Fibonacci combo cluster technique provides trade entry signals where no other means of determination is present. Really?

In Chapter 3, we discussed how useful the closure of Gaps and Laps can be in targeting trade entry, and how an open Gap, an untested Y-Close, represents *unfinished business* to the continuation of a trend. In Figure G.2, the history of gaps apparent in the same data selection has been numbered 1 through 5 for easier viewing.

Had entries been made simply on the basis of gap-closure in the direction of the break-away, using the instrument of DTV for this same period, the stock could have been traded with the precision of a skilled surgeon. No *sacred science* required. If the entry is actually made at the gap closure itself, without any subsequent trend confirmation action, a stop-loss order can be

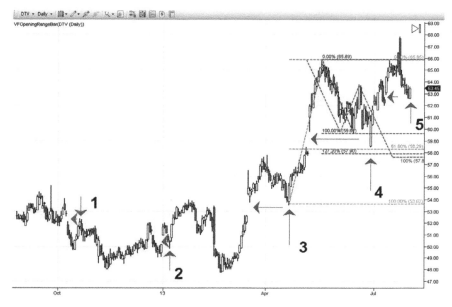

FIGURE G.2 Gap-Close Trade Entries in DTV

nested just beyond the reversal should the impending trend continuation fail to show any significant reversal distance.

Of equal interest in that same webinar was a second example, using the stock of REGN, not shown here, from approximately the same calendar period. This time, a similar Fibonacci combo was drawn into a cluster in an area where no open gap was present. Instead, the cluster confluence met the precise price level of a prominent Pivot Ledge!

I've come back after all these years to the Old School of technical analysis, even though I employ a New School algorithm for the Serial Sequent Wave Method. The Old School delivers an abundance of opportunities that are derived directly from the charts themselves. And furthermore, I would flip around the contention made by that webinar presenter regarding Fibonacci clusters: Special chart pattern recognition methods from the Pivot/Exhaustion Grid identify trade entry levels where Fibonacci methods either fail, or fail to even exist.

FIGURE 6.2 Cap-Zone Trade Entries to DIV

The Last Triangle

Dating back to the Civil War, the Axe-Houghton Industrial Stock Price Average was still in common use before the Dow Jones Industrial Average came into being in the early part of the 1900s. It used a different method of weighting and included a slightly different mix of stocks. It is clear from a study of this index that a long-term bull market cycle, now referred to as a Krondratieff Wave, had been in place since the Panic of 1857, where the Axe-Houghton traded briefly below 10, climbing to a high in late 1919 of just over 210.

From this high in 1919, the Axe-Houghton Industrial Average fell back into a triangle that took nearly five years to complete, as seen in Figure H.1.

On very close examination, in mid-1924, price action briefly made a false breakout to the downside of that triangle. But by the end of the year, prices had successfully reversed and were pushing out the upside of the triangle, back in sync with the long-term bull.

After rallying for more than a year, price broke sharply, and in mid-1926 fell in a straight vertical drop back down to the apex of the triangle, losing 25 percent of its value to around 150. The apex repelled the decline, and for the next three-and-a-half years until October 1929, prices tripled in the biggest stock market rally of all time, reaching 430 in the Axe-Houghton Average.

Any student of history knows the story from there. The decline was swift and steep. In just half the time it took to rally away from the apex of the triangle, the market had returned back down to it a second time. But this time, in mid-1931, the apex did not repel price action as before (terminate-if-touched). The market cut through the apex like a knife through butter,

FIGURE H.1   The Great Crash of 1929

Source: H. M. Gartley, *Profits in the Stock Market* (Pomeroy, WA: Lambert Gann Publishing, 1935).

and in just one more year, the Axe-Houghton was to be cut in half two more times before the final low was made in mid-1932, around 46.25.

The words of my mentor, Randolph Newman, still haunt me whenever I see a triangle. "What tales of timing the triangles tell."

Bartiromo, Maria. *Use the News*. New York: HarperBusiness, 2001.

Bernstein, Peter L. *Against the Gods: The Remarkable Story of Risk*. New York: John Wiley & Sons, 1996.

Brandt, Peter, and Bruce Babcock Jr. *Trading Commodity Futures with Classic Chart Patterns*. Sacramento, CA: Advanced Trading Seminars, Inc., 1990.

Connors, Laurence A., and Linda Bradford Raschke. *Street Smarts*. Los Angeles: M. Gordon Publishing Group, 1996.

Crabel, Toby. *Day Trading with Short Term Price Patterns and Opening Range Breakout*. Greenville, SC: Traders Press, 1990.

Dalton, James, Eric T. Jones, and Robert B. Dalton. *Mind Over Markets*. Greenville, SC: Traders Press, 1999.

Darvas, Nicholas. *How I Made $2,000,000 in the Stock Market*. Larchmont, NY: American Research Council, 1960.

DiNapoli, Joe. *Trading with DiNapoli Levels*. Coast Investment Software, 1998.

Douglas, Mark. *Trading in the Zone*. Chicago, IL: Trading Behavior Dynamics, 1998.

Douglas, Mark. *The Disciplined Trader*. Paramus, NJ: New York Institute of Finance, division of Simon & Schuster, 1990.

Drummond, Charles. *How to Make Money in the Futures Markets and Lots of It*. Bridgewater, N.S., Canada: Charles Drummond Publisher, 1979.

Gartley, H. M. *Profits in the Stock Market*. Pomeroy, WA: Lambert-Gann Publishing, 1935.

Gould, Bruce. *Dow Jones–Irwin Guide to Commodities Trading*. Homewood, IL: Dow Jones–Irwin, 1973.

Hill, John R. *Scientific Interpretation of Bar Charts*. Henderson, NC: Commodity Research Bureau, 1979.

Horney, Karen. *Neurosis and Human Growth: The Struggle Toward Self-Realization*. New York: W. W. Norton & Company, Inc., 1950.

Laffer, Arthur. "So You Thought the Fed Set Interest Rates." *Wall Street Journal*, March 22, 2001.

Levin, Larry. *The Secrets of Floor Traders*. Mt. Prospect, IL: Trading Advantage, 1998.

Marder, Kevin N., and Marc Dupee. *The Best: TradingMarkets.com Conversations with Top Traders*. Los Angeles: M. Gordon Publishing Group, 2000.

Miner, Robert C. *Dynamic Trading*. Tucson, AZ: Dynamic Trading Group, 1996. dynamictraders.com.

Noble, Grant. *The Trader's Edge*. Chicago, IL: Probus Publishing, McGraw-Hill, 1994.

Pesavento, Larry. *The Opening Price Principle: The Best Kept Secret on Wall Street*. Greenville, SC: Traders Press, 1999.

Prechter, Robert, and A. J. Frost. *Elliott Wave Principle*. Gainsville, GA: New Classics Library, 1998.

Raschke, Linda Bradford. *Swing Trading: Rules and Philosophy*. LBR Group, 2001. www.lbrgroup.com.

Raschke, Linda Bradford. *Professional Trading Techniques*. LBR Group, 1998. www.lbr.com.

Ross, Joe. *Trading by the Book*. Freeport G.B. Bahamas: Trading Educators LTD, 1990.

Schabacker, Richard W. *Technical Analysis and Stock Market Profits*. London: Pitman Publishing, 1932.

Schwager, Jack D. *Schwager on Futures, Technical Analysis*. New York: John Wiley & Sons, 1996.

Sperando, Vic. *Trader Vic—Methods of a Wall Street Master*. New York: John Wiley & Sons, 1991.

Steidlmayer, J. Peter, and Kevin Koy. *Markets and Maket Logic*. Chicago: Porcupine Press, 1986.

Steidlmayer, J. Peter. *Steidlmayer on Markets: Trading with Market Profile*. Hoboken, NJ: Wiley Trading, 2002.

Taylor, George Douglass. *The Taylor Trading Technique*. Greenville, SC: Traders Press, 1950.

Tharp, Dr., Van K. *Trade Your Way to Financial Freedom*. New York: McGraw-Hill, 1998.

Wall, P. Q. *Destiny Is Real*. New Orleans: Garden District Publishing, 1999.

Warren, Ted. *How to Make the Stock Market Make Money for You*. Grants Pass, OR: Four Star Books, Inc, 1966.

Williams, Larry. *Long-Term Secrets to Short-Term Trading* New York: John Wiley & Sons, 1999.

Wolfe, Bill. WolfeWave Methodology. www.wolfewave.com.

Will Scheier currently teaches a course on Serial Sequent Wave Method and markets the software for this method and a package of other proprietary indicators through the website ValhallaFutures.com. He also offers real-time futures analysis and trade calls from a free traders chat room online.

Will began his career with the equity and commodity markets as a stockbroker for Bache & Co. in 1979, became a Vice President at A.G. Edwards, Inc., and then left to start his own ventures. He has published market letters, commentary and trade recommendations for his own Introducing Brokerage, as well as for other firms. He has acted as an analyst, a training coach, author, advisor, CTA, and independent trader to the futures and derivatives markets for these many years.

During the course of continual research into trading methodology, Will has studied and mastered most of the better-known authors and method vendors starting with the earliest forerunners of technical analysis, from the "old school" like Charles Dow, Richard Schabacker, W. D. Gann, H. M. Gartley, R. N. Elliott, George Taylor, and Charles Lindsay, through their "middle school" protégés like Joe Granville, Grant Noble, Charles Drummond, Larry Williams, Welles Wilder, Joe Ross, Connie Brown, and Robert Miner. He tries to keep up with those of his peers who offer various methods derivative of either school, or who involve the new school of computer algorithms, like some of his own. However, Will has found few of the methods and authors of technical analysis very helpful in the lower time frames of the intraday stock index futures markets, where he has recognized significant profit opportunities.

Will credits having spent some formative years mentoring with a former cotton trader from New Orleans, and subsequently training on the floor of the S&P pit in its heyday. Subsequently, Will has developed his own trading methods, especially uncovering a method to accurately dissect the internal structure of fractal wave formation, which he calls Serial Sequent Wave Method. Will uses this as a replacement for Elliott Wave, which he finds far too inexact for the identification of reversal and breakout levels in the lower time frames of the volatile index futures.

1-minute time frame, 14–15, 17, 20, 35, 37–39, 50, 66, 75, 92–93, 103, 109, 115, 117, 119, 123, 138, 141, 144, 146, 163–165

1st Frame, 3–4, 6–9, 13, 17, 24, 40, 50, 55, 57, 64, 66, 69, 73, 81–82, 89–91, 93, 96, 103, 106, 108, 112, 118, 125, 127–130, 137, 141–142, 152, 160

1st Trend Direction, 96–97, 99–101

2:30 P.M. Transition Time, 4, 9, 11, 85, 143, 146, 151

2nd Trend Direction, 96, 98, 100–101, 136, 154, 177

3-Bar ORB, 15–16, 18

3-day cycle, 84, 105–106, 110, 135–136, 139, 158

10-minute time frame, 33, 115–117, 119, 163, 165

10:30 A.M. Trend Check, 4, 12, 64, 66, 83, 85, 99, 127, 151, 159–160, 168, 170

60-minute time frame, 38–39, 45, 164–167, 188, 198

89EMA, 38, 93, 142, 147, 187

200EMA, 38, 66, 91–93, 141–147, 170–171, 187

1300EMA, 39, 66, 170, 188

1300SMA, 188

A

Accountant, The, 174–176

all-session, 32, 40–41, 45–46, 165, 167, 188, 196, 198

amateur hour, 13

Analyst, The, 11, 23, 97, 173–176, 198

apex, 43, 65, 99, 130, 170, 207

Axe-Houghton Industrial Average, 130, 207

B

behavior, xii, 3–4, 9, 11, 29, 63–64, 81, 93, 103, 126, 128–129, 139, 145, 151, 158, 172, 174, 178–180, 182–183

black line color code, 27, 164, 188; see also mnemonic memory device

blog, 181, 183

blue line color code, 32, 163, 187, 203; see also mnemonic memory device

blueprint, 176, 179

Book Method, 105

bracket, brackets, 14, 18–19, 24, 46, 69, 99, 182, 188, 196

Break-away Lap, 28–31, 38, 73, 164, 188:
  defined, 28
  plotted, 29
  retested, 30
  as *unfinished business* 31

Break-away Pivot, 27, 30, 42, 46, 63, 74, 99, 188; see also Pivot Ledge

break-even, 37, 124, 132, 180

breakout trigger, 146, 164, 172

brown line color code, 39, 187–188; see also mnemonic memory device

Buy Day, 105, 110, 134

C

center line, 43, 66, 138–139

channel, 43, 46, 66, 70, 122, 136–139, 142, 165, 171–172, 193

channel center line, 138

characteristic gesture, 17–18, 85

color legend, line plots, 187–189; see also mnemonic memory device

confluence, 23, 32, 35, 43, 64, 66, 149, 152, 154, 156–170, 172, 174, 176, 178, 180, 182, 184, 193, 197, 205

consolidation, 4, 10, 64, 82, 86, 93, 104, 110, 121, 123, 125, 127, 146, 151, 170, 192

contract management, 18, 37

corollary, 55, 98, 131–132, 138, 142

Corollary #1, 98, 142

Corollary #2, 132, 138

CQG, 40, 47

Cup, The, 93, 101, 144–147, 166:
   as Breakout Trigger, 146

Cup-n-Saucer, 166

cyan line color code, 32, 187; see also mnemonic memory device

D

Daily Blog, 181, 183

Daily Journal, 176, 181, 183–184

Daily Pivot Point, DP, 40, 156, 187; see also pivot points

Day Model Pattern, 22:
   Day Model Sequence Cycle, 105–112
   Persistent Trend Day, 21, 81–93
   Split-Open Day, 81–82, 101, 103–104
   Test-and-Reject Day, 81–82, 95–102

Day Model Sequence, 92, 100, 105, 107, 109, 111, 134–135, 143, 147, 169, 177:
   Taylor's 3-day Cycle, 106, 110
   Taylor's Sell Day, 110
   Taylor's Short Day, 110

day-session, day-only, 32, 34, 39–41, 45–46, 187–188, 196

Declining/Rising Wedge, 134–136, 166

derivatives, 40, 63, 105, 125, 182, 193, 199

diagonal triangle, 134

Die Bar, 49–51, 53–54, 73, 142; see also Dough Bar

disparate, 35, 45, 66, 157, 159, 161

divergence, 46, 55, 57–59, 61, 64, 66, 75, 87, 91, 118, 163, 165, 177

Dough Bar, 49–51, 53–54, 73, 142; see also Die Bar

Douglas Premise, 97–98, 102, 131–132, 138, 142

Douglas, Mark, 97, 101–102

Dow 30, mini, YM, futures contract, 16–17, 55, 66, 75, 82, 102, 157, 207

DP, Daily Pivot Point, 40, 156, 187; see also Floor Trader's Pivots

dynamic exhaustion, 37

E

E-mini, 16–17, 34, 55, 66

E-mini S&P, 16, 55, 66

economic news, 69, 160

Efficient Market Theory, 108

Elliott, R. N., 191, 193:
   Elliott *abc* pattern, 9

Elliott Wave, 41, 47, 158, 191–192, 214

89EMA Entry, 141–147

EMA Cup, 144–145, 147

EMA Pinch, 141

EMA, exponential moving average, 37–39, 141–142, 144–147

ending triangles, 130

ES, E-mini S&P 500 futures contract, 16, 27–28, 39, 55–57, 59, 62, 90, 108, 132, 152, 159–163, 167–168, 170, 183

eSignal, 40–41, 47

Event Concept, 65

Event Model, 158, 163–166, 168, 170–172, 180–182, 193, 197–198

excursion, 42–43, 67, 111, 119, 122, 166–167, 172, 192

execution, 96, 125, 127, 139, 149, 152, 154, 156, 158, 160, 162, 164, 166, 168, 170, 172, 174–176, 178, 180, 182, 184

exhaustion, 23–25, 27, 29, 31–35, 37–39, 41, 43, 45–47, 141, 144, 158–161, 165, 167, 170, 177, 182, 187, 189, 203, 205; see also Pivot/Exhaustion Grid

extension, 41, 158, 192, 203

F

Federal Reserve, 108

Fibonacci, 35, 41–43, 46, 158, 203–205:
   targets, 41–43

Cluster of Three Methods, 204
Inverse 78.6% Projection Rule, 42
vs. Pivot/Exhaustion Grid, 203–205
1-minute time frame, 14–15, 17, 20, 35, 37–39,
  50, 66, 75, 92–93, 103, 109, 115, 117,
  119, 123, 138, 141, 144, 146, 163–165
1st Frame, 3–4, 6–9, 13, 17, 24, 40, 50, 55,
  57, 64, 66, 69, 73, 81–82, 89–91,
  93, 96, 103, 106, 108, 112, 118, 125,
  127–130, 137, 141–142, 152, 160
1st Trend Direction, 96–97, 99–101
Telltale Triangles, 128–129
Floor Trader's Pivots, 40, 156, 187; see also
  pivot points
Flubber Bounce/Monkey Bars, 89, 91–92

G

Gap, 13, 28–30, 34–35, 40, 46, 50–51, 56, 59,
  65, 71, 83, 98, 100, 108–111, 118,
  127, 134, 143–144, 159, 167, 170,
  188, 204–205
Gap Chart, 46
Gap-Close, 34–35, 51, 143, 205
Gap-Close Trade Entries in DTV, 205
Gap-n-go, 34–35, 83, 144
Globex High/Low, 32–33, 100, 196
Great Crash of 1929, 208
green line color code, 14, 38, 115–116, 119,
  187, 203; see also mnemonic memory
  device

H

Head-and-Shoulders, 43, 66, 101, 127,
  131–132, 136:
  inverse, 127
  neckline vs target considerations, 133
Heraclitus, 1, 33, 79, 89, 113, 136, 149, 183
high frequency trading, 125, 127
HOD, High-of-Day, 66, 75, 162–164, 169; see
  also LOD, Low-of-Day

I

indicator, 6, 12, 27, 29, 32, 37, 39–41, 44, 46,
  71, 115–117, 119, 142, 163, 184, 193,
  195–196, 198
Indicator Package, 12, 46, 116, 195
Intraday Index Futures Trading Course,
  195–196

intuition, 4, 44, 64, 66, 90, 174–175, 180–181,
  183
Inverse 78% Projection Rule, 42, 66, 170–172
Inverse Head-and-Shoulders, 101, 127, 131

J

journal, 176, 181, 183–184

K

Kilroy, 24–26, 163, 171
Krondratieff Wave, 207

L

Lane, George, 115
Lap, 28–31, 36–38, 65, 73, 164, 188
Last Chance Texaco, 86, 91–93, 142
Last Hour Time Frame, 3–4, 9–10, 57, 91,
  142, 154
Last Triangle, 207–208
leadership, 55–57, 59–62, 75, 85–90, 109,
  163:
  divergence, 56
  Serial Divergence, 57–58
  TF Divergence, 56
  TF Divergence Payoff, 58, 59
  TF Lagging or Leading?, 61
Leadership Shift, 59, 61–62, 87, 89
Levin, Larry, 93
liquidity, 56
LOD, Low-of-Day, 66, 75, 162–164, 169; see
  also HOD, High-of-Day

M

M-Top Pattern, (W-Bottom), 101, 127, 146,
  152
MA Pattern Concepts, 93, 141, 143, 145, 147:
  Cup as Breakout Trigger, 146
  89EMA Entry, 141–147
  EMA Pinch, 141–147
  EMA Cup, 144–147
  Gap-Close, 143–144
  200EMA Entry, 141–147
Market Profile®, 43, 47
Measured Move, 43, 46, 66, 132, 136, 139,
  171–172:
  targets, 43
mechanical behavior governors, 178, 180–182

mentor, 11, 55, 76, 97–98, 129, 173

Midday Channel, 43, 136–138, 171–172:
 Douglas Premise and, 138
 midpoint, 38–39
 overview, 136–139
 Persistent Trend and, 139
 Pre-Breakout Pause Pattern and, 138
 Test-and-Reject Day and, 136

Midday Frame, 3–4, 7–10, 15, 36, 66, 69, 89, 91, 93, 103, 123, 127–129, 136, 142, 145, 164, 177:
 transition, 7–8
 trending, 9
 volatility, 8

midpoint, 38–39; see also Midday Channel

Millennium bull, 130

Miner, Robert, 41, 203

mini Russell 2000 futures contract, TF, 16–17, 34, 37, 51, 55–57, 66, 86–87, 109

mini-channel, 122

mnemonic memory device, for line plots, 24, 32–34, 187–188:
 black line color code, 27, 164, 188
 blue line color code, 32, 163, 187, 203
 brown line color code, 39, 187–188
 cyan line color code, 32, 187
 green line color code, 14, 38, 115–116, 119, 187, 203
 orange line color code, 29, 164, 188
 red line color code, 14, 34, 101, 128, 163, 165, 188
 yellow line color code, 33, 188, 199

momentum, 4, 23, 65, 84, 115, 117–119, 142, 144, 158, 163, 165, 168–170, 177, 196

Momentum Grid, 115, 117, 119:
 completed Stochastic Split Signal, 117
 momentum turns before price, 117–118
 1-minute stochastic line, 117, 119
 Period D 7, 115
 Period K 14, 115
 Persistent Trend Day and, 119, 120
 Smoothing 3, 115
 Split-Open Model and, 115–116, 118, 120
 Stochastic Grid and, 115
 stochastic oscillator, 115–116
 Stochastic Split and, 116–117
 StochSplit Signal, 118–120
 Test-and-Reject reversal opportunity, 117–118, 120

Monkey Bars/Flubber Bounce, 89–90, 92

MyPivots.com, 41, 44

N

Narrow Range Day Signal, 104

neckline, 43, 131–133; see also Head-and-Shoulders

New School, 77, 125, 193, 205

Newman, Randolph, 11, 55, 76, 79, 113, 129, 149, 199, 201

news release, 69, 71, 76

Ninjacharts, 47, 116, 196; see also Ninjatrader.com

Ninjatrader, 46, 116, 158, 178, 182, 189, 195–196

Noble, Grant, 6, 12, 93, 104

Noon Hour High/Low/Pullback, 57, 66, 83, 85, 115, 151–152, 154–155, 163, 165–166, 171, 177:
 Trade Entry Model, 163, 165
 transition time reversals, 154–155

NQ, E-mini Nasdaq 100 index futures contract, 16–17, 29, 39, 55, 59, 75, 108–109, 115, 152, 159–164, 170, 183

nuclear, 18, 21, 85

O

OCO, 178, 182

Old School, 40, 126, 159, 193, 205

1-Minute Bar, 92:
 stochastic line, Momentum Grid and, 117, 119
 time bars, 38
 6-tick bars as microscope of, 37
 60-minute frame MAs from within 1-minute bars, 39

Opening Range Bar, ORB, 13–22, 24–26, 33, 38, 46, 49–51, 59, 65, 71, 75, 81–83, 85–86, 89–90, 92–93, 95–96, 99–101, 103, 109–110, 115, 117–118, 123, 127, 151–152, 159–160, 163, 166, 168–169, 171–172, 177, 188:
 defined, 13–15
 Dough/Die Bar and, 49–50
 ORB Kilroy, 24–26
 ORB Matched Highs/Lows, 20–21
 ORB Pennant, 17–20
 support and resistance throughout day as, 14
 3-Bar ORB, 15–17

orange line color code, 29, 164, 188; see also mnemonic memory device
ORB Kilroy, 24:
  containing action, 25
  trend correction, exhaustion of, 25
ORB Matched Highs/Lows, 20:
  Matched Highs ORB setup and breakout, 20–21
ORB Pennant, 17–20, 85–86, 99:
  Persistent Trend Day and, 85–86
  setup and breakout, 18
  Test-and-Reject Day, 99
  variation of, 19
oscillator, 83, 115

P

pennant, 17–20, 85–86, 99, 122, 170, 172
Period D, 115–116
Period K, 115
persistence, 82–83, 90–91, 95, 107, 110
Persistent Trend Day, 21, 62, 81–87, 89, 91–93, 95–96, 98, 100–101, 105–106, 108–112, 119, 126–127, 129, 134–136, 139, 141–145, 151, 154, 164–165, 168–170:
  Day Model Sequence Cycle and, 105–112
  Flubber Bounce, 89–91
  Last Chance Texaco, 86, 91–93
  leadership, 85–89
  Leadership Shift, 87–89
  Midday Channel and, 139
  Midday Frame, 89
  Momentum Grid and, 119, 120
  Monkey Bars, 89–91
  ORB Pennant and, 85–86
  overview, 82–85
  pullback entry opportunities in the laggards, 87
  recapture of leadership, 88
  Telltale leadership, 85–86
  transition time reversals, 151, 154
  200EMA Entry, 91–93, 141
Philly Fed, 69, 71
Pivot/Exhaustion Grid, 41:
  Break-away Lap, 28–31
  Break-away Pivots, 27–28
  day-only session, 32
  Dynamic Exhaustion Levels, 37–39
  EMAs, 37–39
  Fibonacci Targets, 41–43

  vs. Fibonacci Targets, 203–205
  Floor Trader's Pivot Points, 40–41
  Gap, 34–35
  Gap–Closes, 34–35
  Globex High/Low, 32–34
  Market Profile, 43–44
  Measured Move targets, 43
  Pivot Ledge, 27–28
  Point of Control (POC), 43–44
  previous closing prices, 34–35
  previous highs and lows, 31–34
  Y-High/Lows/Close, 33–35
  symmetrical triangle apex, 43
  terminate-if-touched, 32
  Tick Bar Laps, 35–37
  trend lines, 44–46
Pivot Ledge, 27–31, 36–38, 42–43, 46, 71, 73, 75, 160, 170–171, 188:
  plotted, 27
  retested, 28
pivot points, 40; see also Floor Trader's Pivots
Pivot/Exhaustion Grid, 23, 25, 27, 29, 31–33, 35, 37–39, 41, 43, 45–47, 158, 165, 187, 189, 203, 205
Point of Control, POC, 43–44, 46
position management strategies and methods, Trade Plan, 178–179, 182–183
position trading, xi–xii, 7, 46
Post-Breakout Pause, 123–124, 128
Pre-Breakout Pause, 121–124, 129, 134, 138, 143, 146, 154, 156, 170, 172, 177, 180
Prechter, Robert, 41
prescript, Trade Plan, 174
Projection Rule, Inverse 78%, 42, 171–172

R

R1, R2, R3, S1, S2, S3, DP, 40; see also pivot points
Random Walk, xii
Raschke, Linda Bradford, 105, 112, 115, 120
red line color code, 14, 34, 101, 128, 163, 165, 188; see also mnemonic memory device
repetitive chart patterns:
  classics, 125–140
  MA Pattern Concepts, 141–147
  Momentum Grid, 115–120
  Pre-Breakout Pause Pattern, 121–124
resolution, 4, 10
retracement, 41, 97, 119, 203

Rising/Declining Wedge, 134–136, 166
runner, 21, 37, 110, 128, 166, 178, 183
Running Correction, 136

S

S1, S2, S3, R1, R2, R3, DP, 40; see also pivot
    points
S&P 500, 3, 6
Screen Capturing an Event Library, 197–198
2nd Trend Direction, 96, 98, 100–101, 136,
    154, 177
Sell Day, Taylor Book Method, 105, 110
Sell Short Day, Taylor Book Method, 105
sequence cycle, 92, 105, 107, 109, 111, 134,
    143, 147, 172
Serial Divergence, 57–58
Serial Sequent Wave Method, 46, 77, 158, 177,
    191–193, 195–196, 205, 214
Settlement Close, 40, 104
setup, 10, 15–21, 33, 43, 70–72, 74, 86–87,
    108, 123–124, 131–132
shoulder, Head-and-Shoulders, 27–29,
    131–133, 152, 163
6-tick bars as microscope of 1-minute bars, 37
60-minute frame MAs from within 1-minute
    bars, 39
SMA, Simple Moving Average, 39, 170
smoothing, 115
Solo New High/Low (HOD/LOD), 66, 75,
    162–164, 169
Split-Open Day, 81–82, 101, 103–104,
    115–116, 120:
    Narrow Range Day Signal, 104
Stochastic Split, StochSplit, 116–120, 163, 165,
    168, 170
stop-entry, 18, 69–70, 138, 164, 168
SuperDom, 178
support/resistance, 14, 24–25, 27, 38–40, 43–44,
    66, 83, 95, 103, 146, 164, 177, 182
swing, xii–xiii, 13, 25, 27, 51, 64, 67, 82,
    89–90, 100–101, 110, 112, 134,
    160–161, 172, 182, 185
Symmetrical Triangle, 43

T

tape reading, 44, 64, 66, 90, 174–175, 180, 183
target, 16, 36–37, 41–43, 49, 51, 54, 56, 64,
    66, 70, 74–75, 85, 92, 99, 103, 119,
    132–134, 136, 138–139, 152, 159,
    161, 170–172, 178:
    Head-and-Shoulders reversals, 133
Taylor Book Method, 105:
    3-day Cycle, 106, 110
    Sell Day, 110
    Short Day, 110
Taylor, George Douglass, 84, 93, 105, 112
Technical Event, xii, 35, 158, 161, 172, 179,
    193, 198
Technical Trade Entry Model, 64, 66
tell, 84–85, 109, 113, 129, 131, 136–137, 179
Telltale, 28, 63, 85, 127, 136:
    leadership, Persistent Trend Day, 85–86
    triangles, 127–131
10:30 Trend Check, 4, 12, 64, 66, 83, 85, 99,
    127, 151, 159–160:
    Trade Entry Model, 159–160, 170, 171
    transition time reversals, 152–154
terminate-if-touched, 32, 187–189,
    195–196
Test-and-Reject Day, 82, 95–97, 99–101, 103,
    106, 108–110, 117–118, 120–121, 124,
    126, 128–129, 134, 136, 140, 144, 146,
    152, 154, 168, 170–171, 177:
    Douglas Premise, 97–98, 102
    generally, 140
    ORB Breakout, 95
    ORB Pennant, 99
    Telltale Triangles, 128
    Trade Entry Model, 171
    transition time reversals and, 152
    W-Bottoms and, 126
    Work-Done, 97–99
TF, mini Russell 2000 futures contract, 16–17,
    25, 29, 34–35, 38–39, 45, 55–62, 72–
    73, 75, 86, 88, 90, 98–99, 108–109,
    128, 132, 163–168, 170, 182:
    divergence, 56
    divergence payoff, 58, 59
    lagging or leading, 61
    leadership payoff, 60
    Leadership Shift, 61
    Pre-News trade entry setup/payoff, 72–73
1300EMA, 39, 66, 170, 188
1300SMA, 188
Three-Day Cycle, 3-Day Cycle, 84, 105–106,
    110, 135–136, 139, 158; see also Taylor
    Book Method

INDEX

3rd (Last Hour Time Frame), 3, 9–10:
    89EMA Entry, 142
    leadership divergence, 57
    transition, 9–10
3-Bar ORB, 15–17:
    bear setup with breakout, 16
    valid/invalid setup examples, 17
3-Minute Bars, 36
Tick Bar Laps, 35
Time Marker, 10, 12, 83, 85, 99, 151, 154,
        161, 166–167, 170, 177:
    Trade Entry Model, 161, 167
    transition time reversals and, 152
trade entry, 4, 6, 14, 24, 33, 35–36, 38, 42–43,
        45–46, 54, 64, 66, 70, 72, 74, 81, 89,
        96, 101, 111–112, 119, 121, 127, 131,
        141, 146, 152, 156–161, 163–165,
        167, 169, 171–172, 175, 180,
        182–183, 193, 203–205
Trade Entry Model, 43, 54, 64, 66, 89, 152,
        157, 161, 164–165, 167, 172, 175,
        183, 193, 203
Trade Model Criteria, Trade Plan, 177, 179–181
Trade Plan, 4, 36, 44, 64, 66, 70, 73, 98, 123,
        164, 172–177, 179–181, 183–184, 198:
    Accountant role, 174
    Analyst role, 174–176
    author's Blueprint Notes, 179–183
    Blue Print, 176–183
    Mechanical Behavior Governors, 178,
        180–182
    Position Management Strategies and
        Methods, 178–179, 182–183
    Prescript, 174–176
    Trade Model Criteria, 177, 179–181
trade simulator, 180, 183
Trader, The, xiii, 8, 11, 37, 51, 54, 63–64, 74,
        85–86, 89, 92, 95, 97–98, 101, 115,
        120, 123–124, 126–127, 130–132, 136,
        138, 140–141, 151–152, 157, 161, 164,
        167–168, 170–172, 174–176, 179–180,
        187, 191–193, 197, 203
Trader's Edge (Noble), 6, 104
trading range, 7, 38, 64, 108, 147, 160, 177
Trading the news:
    Post-News Trade Model, 75
    Post-News Trade Payoff, 76
    Serial Sequent Wave Method, 77
trampoline bounce, 200EMA Entry, 144

Transition Times, 4–5, 12, 66, 85, 101, 158:
    defined, 4–5
    Breakouts, 153, 154
    Noon Hour, 154–155
    Persistent Trend Day and, 151, 154
    price swings, 152
    10:30 Trend Check, 152–154
    Time Markers, 152
trend, xi–xii, 3–4, 6–10, 14–16, 18–19, 21–22,
        24–27, 31–34, 37–38, 42–46, 49–51,
        56–57, 59, 62–64, 66–67, 69–71,
        73–74, 76, 81–87, 89–93, 95–101,
        103–112, 117–131, 134–145, 147,
        151–161, 164–172, 177, 179, 182, 188,
        191–193, 196, 204–205
trend line, 45–46, 128, 134, 164–167, 188
    All-Session, 60-minute charts, 45
    Gap Chart, 46
triangles, 113, 127–131
trip, the, 25, 34, 36, 65–66, 95, 116–121,
        144, 147
20/20 auto-screen capture preferences, 198
2:30 Transition Time, Trade Entry Model, 166
200EMA Entry, 91–93, 141–147:
    1-minute bars, 92
    spike reversal, 145
    Trade Entry Model, 170
    trampoline bounce, 144

U

unfinished business, 30–31, 36, 43, 46, 63, 73,
        130, 204

V

valhallafutures.com, 12, 47, 181, 183, 193,
        196:
    Indicator Package, 46–47, 195–196
Value Area, 43–44, 65
volatility:
    1st frame, 3, 6
    Midday Frame, 8

W

W-Bottom Pattern (M-Top), 101, 126–127,
        163, 168
Website, companion, 185
Work-Done, 63–67, 96, 98–101, 134, 159,
        161, 172

Y

Y-Close (Yesterday's Close), 14, 29, 32, 34–35, 40, 64–65, 73, 100, 144, 167, 188, 204
Y-High, 32, 34, 40, 64–65, 188; see also Y-Close (Yesterday's Close)
Y-Low, 14, 29, 32, 34–35, 40, 64–65, 73, 100, 144, 167, 188, 204; see also Y-Close (Yesterday's Close)

yellow line color code, 33, 188, 199; see also mnemonic memory device
YM, mini Dow 30 futures contract, 16–17, 25, 29, 39, 55, 62, 75, 100, 108, 164–166, 170, 183

Printed and bound by CPI Group (UK) Ltd, Croydon, CR0 4YY

16/04/2025

14658446-0003